Style and Stylistics

CONCEPTS OF LITERATURE

GENERAL EDITOR: WILLIAM RIGHTER

Department of English
University of Warwick

Style and Stylistics

by Graham Hough

Professor of English Literature
University of Cambridge

LONDON
ROUTLEDGE & KEGAN PAUL
NEW YORK: HUMANITIES PRESS

First published in 1969
by Routledge & Kegan Paul Ltd
Broadway House, 68–74 Carter Lane
London E.C.4
Printed in Great Britain
by Willmer Brothers Limited
SBN 7100 6416 0 (C)
SBN 7100 6417 9 (P)

General Editor's Introduction

The study of literature has normally centred on the consideration of work, author, or historical period. But increasingly there is a demand for a more analytic approach, for investigation and explanation of literary concepts of crucial ideas and issues—topics which are of general importance to the critical consideration of particular works. This series undertakes to provide a clear description and critical evaluation of such important ideas as 'symbolism', 'realism', 'style' and other terms used in literary discussion. It also undertakes to define the relationship of literature to other intellectual disciplines: anthropology, philosophy, psychology, etc., for it is in connection with such related fields that much important recent critical work has been done. *Concepts of Literature* will both account for the methodology of literary study, and will define its dimensions by reference to the many activities that throw light upon it. Individual works will describe the fundamental outlines of particular problems and explore the frontiers that they suggest. The series as a whole will provide a survey of recent literary thought.

It is often claimed that stylistic study using linguistic methods may provide a new intellectual discipline for literary criticism. Professor Hough examines the claims of stylistics, in a variety of its forms, to determine both its benefits and its limitations. His is consciously a literary approach, continually asking, 'How does this method advance our understanding of particular literary works, or in a wider context, of the phenomenon of literature itself?' His scepticism about quantitative analysis is not due to any hostility towards scientific procedures in their own right, but rather to his rigorous questioning of the criteria of what is relevant in any given literary case. The resulting appraisal has important bearings on the scope and character of the critic's task.

WILLIAM RIGHTER

Contents

I would maintain that to formulate observation by means of words is not to cause the artistic beauty to evaporate in vain intellectualities; rather, it makes for a widening and deepening of the aesthetic taste. It is only a frivolous love that cannot survive intellectual definition; great love prospers with understanding.

LEO SPITZER

Preface

The object of this essay is to give a short account of the
modern study of literary style. It is necessarily selective
and incomplete, but I have tried to indicate the main
directions that such work has taken, and the directions
it might take in the future. Style-study has often grown
from linguistics, sometimes from other starting-points.
But whatever its origin, stylistics is inevitably a study of
language. The only matter for dispute is how literary
language should be studied. Linguistics is by now a formidable and autonomous discipline, and its relation with
literary studies has not been easy. Many of its concerns
are irrelevant to literature, and some of its methods are
disliked by most literary students. Yet in the end it cannot
be irrelevant. The study of language and the study of
literature obviously have a common frontier, and stylistics is the border area.

This book is written from the literary point of view.
I hope what I have said will not seem positively wrong
to professional linguists; but it is not my aim to satisfy
their demands or their criteria of relevance. I have not
tried to inquire how linguistics could revolutionize the
study of literature, but how much it can contribute to the

study of literature as that is ordinarily understood. A subsidiary aim has been to bring together Continental work in stylistics and English work which, though it has never been called 'stylistics', has actually the same object. There is something to be gained by seeing them in the same perspective.

I should like to thank Peter Seuren, of Darwin College and the Cambridge Department of Linguistics, for kindly reading my typescript and clarifying some linguistic matters that were very dimly present to my consciousness.

Darwin College   G.H.
Cambridge

1

The concept of style and the origins of style-study

Older Concepts of Style

It is a paradox that the term 'style' has tended to disappear from the main stream of modern criticism, while a quasi-independent study of 'stylistics' has simultaneously made its appearance. If we look into the causes of this we shall go far towards defining the rationale of the modern study of literary style.

The concept of style is an old one; it goes back to the very beginnings of literary thought in Europe. It appears in connection with rhetoric rather than poetic, and there seems to be no special reason for this, except that style is regarded as part of the technique of persuasion and therefore discussed largely under the head of oratory. Ancient rhetoric distinguished between ceremonial, political and forensic oratory, and each has its own appropriate occasion and appropriate repertory of devices. If you wish to produce *this* particular effect *these* are the means to bring it about; the proper vocabulary, type of syntax and figures of speech can be prescribed for the purpose in hand (Aristotle, *Rhetoric*, Bk. III; Quintilian, *Institutes of Oratory*, Bk. VIII). The tone of this ancient rhetoric is largely prescriptive—the giving of instructions for appropriate and effective composition. Even a writer like

Longinus, who is much concerned with the moral and spiritual sources of 'the sublime', still goes on to detail the rhetorical figures by which it can be achieved. Ancient rhetoric in its later phases tended to enlarge its discussion to historians and other prose writers. In the Middle Ages and the Renaissance this immense body of rhetorical precept was largely incorporated into poetic, where it had a deep influence not only on critical ideas, but, as recent studies have shown, on the composition of poetry itself. The tradition carries on a lingering existence even into the eighteenth century.

But for us all this is a vanished history. Prescriptive criticism has not been a central literary activity for the last 300 years. In a post-Romantic age it survives only in odd corners—schools of journalism, classes in 'creative writing'. Modern literary study does not presume to dictate to poets; it does not offer instructions towards the forming of a style, it examines styles that are already formed. It is parallel in this respect to linguistic study, which no longer lays down rules for correct grammar, but studies the rules that are actually adhered to by particular cultural groups. The aim is not to give laws for human utterance, but to understand the utterances that actually occur. We can conceive a time when linguistics and criticism might resume their legislative role; but except in countries where literature is decisively subordinated to political necessity this is remote from any currently active way of thinking, and we shall not consider it further.

However, there are other legacies from the old rhetorical concept of style that cannot be dismissed so easily. It was fundamental in traditional rhetoric and criticism to make a separation between matter and manner, what is said and the way of saying it. Such things are often spoken of in metaphor, perhaps necessarily so; and here the commonest metaphor is to speak of language as the dress of thought. Thought is imagined as existing in some pre-verbal form, and it is then *clothed* in language. We can illustrate this from a passage in Dryden's *Preface to Annus Mirabilis*:

So then the first happiness of the poet's imagination is properly invention, or finding of the thought; the second is fancy, or the variation, deriving or moulding of that thought, as the judgment represents it proper to the subject; the third is elocution, or the art of clothing or adorning that thought so found and varied in apt, significant and sounding words.

On this theory it is easy to see what style is. Language is the dress of thought, and style (often, following Quintilian, referred to as 'elocution') is the particular cut and fashion of the dress.

This way of thinking has a number of consequences. The cut or fashion can be looked at from different points of view. Dryden sees it as mainly dictated by the subject; the thought must be moulded in a manner 'proper to the subject'; the words must be 'apt' to the subject. This is in conformity with the general neo-classic theory of literary kinds. Each genre has its own appropriate style; the style of a tragedy is not to be the same as that of a pastoral because they have different subject-matters; and this is nothing to do with the private tastes of the author, but part of the nature of things. At a rather later date, with the advent of expressive theories of literature, style is seen as largely dictated by the nature of the author himself. It is the expression of his personality. *Le style c'est l'homme même*, as we always say in this context, perverting Buffon to our own purpose. By an extension of this approach we can go on to talk about the style of a period or a literary school. But from then on it begins to be doubtful whether we can stay within the limits of the old metaphor—language as the dress of thought. Is the style of the Romantic poets different from that of the school of Pope because they were saying the same things in different ways, or because they were saying different things? Probably the latter; and the more we reflect on it the more doubtful it becomes how far we can talk about *different ways of saying*; is not each different way of saying in fact the saying of a different thing?

The process of reflecting on this subject goes on intermittently through the eighteenth century. Gray could write to his friend Mason in 1762, of a passage in one of his odes: 'It is flat, it is prose.... If the sentiment must stand, twirl it a little into an apophthegm, stick a flower in it, gild it with a costly expression, let it strike the fancy, the ear or the heart, and I am satisfied.'

This is apt to make a post-Romantic generation shudder. If Mason's sentiment was flat, we feel, no amount of gilt or costly expression is going to improve it. By the time we reach the criticism of our own day we find that this whole distinction between matter and manner has been decisively rejected. To reject it has indeed become one of the principal dogmas of current critical thought. The work of literary art is seen as an organic unity, in which matter and manner, thought and expression are indissolubly one; and what began perhaps as an aesthetic doctrine is equally prevalent in considering non-literary utterance. Bloomfield, in an article on 'Linguistic Aspects of Science', says: 'It is a well-tried hypothesis of linguistics that formally different utterances always differ in meaning.' Some recent developments in generative grammar make this look at least doubtful, and the status of synonymy is still open to discussion. But Bloomfield's point of view is still general. On this

THE CONCEPT OF STYLE

hypothesis we cannot talk about different ways of expressing the same thought, but only of different thoughts. What then has become of style? It seems to have disappeared. The case has been put very clearly by Richard M. Ohmann (*Style in Prose Fiction*, 2):

For if style does not have to do with ways of saying *something*, just as style in tennis has to do with ways of hitting a ball, is there anything at all which is worth naming 'style'? ... The critic can talk about what the writer says, but talk about the style he cannot, for his neat identity— one thought, one form—allows no margin for individual variation, which is what we ordinarily mean by style. Style, then, becomes a useless hypothetical construct.

And it is for this reason that the word 'style' makes very little appearance in the main stream of modern criticism.

The Modern Concept of Style

Whatever has happened to the word, however, the concept of style cannot in practice be simply evaporated; for the kind of considerations that used to shelter under its name are still critically active. In England and America there is a huge complex of critical and educational practice that, without using the name, relies largely on stylistic analysis. The experiments in 'practical criticism' conducted by I. A. Richards in the twenties; what is, or was, called the New Criticism in America; the widespread techniques of 'explication' or 'close reading' of poetry— these are all cases in point. The idea that the nature of a whole work can be deduced from the qualities exhibited in a short passage is still widely current; and this is a stylistic dogma. Indeed, all that body of modern criticism which prides itself on its close contact with the verbal texture of literature is a kind of style-study. But the modern critic does not talk about style any more than he talks about beauty. Because the word is out of fashion and the concept now ill-defined, it has been felt necessary to invent new terminologies, and to be excessively cautious about relapsing into old doctrines now regarded as heresies. If we could continue to talk about style—without bringing in undesired and outmoded connotations—it would be an obvious simplification. It would also have the advantage of enlisting at least a little aid from the linguistic disciplines to a kind of criticism that has often had no discipline at all.

In general the linguists seem to have been little embarrassed by the difficulties we have been considering. In spite of the dictum of Bloomfield quoted above, many students of linguistics who have concerned themselves with style are quite content to talk about different ways of saying the same thing. Charles Bally, one of the founding fathers of modern stylistics, defined it as the study of the 'affective' elements in language—these affective elements being conceived as optional additions to an already determinate meaning. More recently Hockett's *Course in Modern Linguistics* asserts that 'two utterances in the same language which convey approximately the same information, but which are different in their linguistic structure, can be said to differ in style: *He came too soon* and *He arrived prematurely*'. Stephen Ullmann quotes a sentence of Proust, then offers a rearranged version of it and says, 'Both sentences mean the same thing.' He goes on to analyse the difference between them as a matter of effectiveness—effectiveness in expressing a given meaning—thus following precisely the definition of style he has quoted earlier from Stendhal: '*ajouter à une pensée donnée toutes les circonstances propres à produire tout l'effet que doit produire cette pensée*'.

The attitude of professional linguistics to this problem is perhaps in process of modification. Late developments of Chomsky's generative grammar have led to the hypothesis (it is yet only a hypothesis) that the deep structure of sentences may be the universal semantic basis of all languages, that they assume different grammatical forms in different languages, and that a single semantic complex in an individual language may indeed assume different but synonymous grammatical forms. The differences between synonymous sentences may then be called stylistic; in fact, a return to the old view of language as the dress of thought. Both the state of the case and the limitations of my knowledge forbid further discussion of the question here.

So I shall not meddle any further with the philosophical or linguistic aspects of the 'one thought, one form' doctrine—not from lack of interest, but from lack of competence. I would claim too that the literary critic has the right to borrow Occam's razor, and may legitimately shear off a good many entities that are not necessary to his purpose. Among them are all discussions about forms of propositions, their relation to the syntactical forms of sentences, and most of what is said about the meaning of meaning. Such considerations occur at a level of abstraction where literary criticism has difficulty in following, where it has no contribution to make and no competence to decide. In these matters the critic may be a probabilist, and use for his purposes any doctrine decently attested by a reputable authority. The value of his conclusions is to be judged by their success in interpreting literature, not by the nature of the non-literary tools he has used on the way.

I think the concept of style can be rescued in three ways, none of them obviously disreputable.

(1) The critic can rest on ordinary language and re-

ceived opinion, 'the common sense of readers uncorrupted by literary prejudice'. Such readers obstinately persevere in distinguishing between matter and manner, the thing said and the way of saying it. The end of literature is to come home to men's business and bosoms, and it can be argued that it is best discussed in the terms in which men's business is normally conducted, to which their bosoms normally return an echo. There is no need to prove that there 'is' such a thing as style; it is enough that it is a convenient and natural term to use, and that in practice everybody knows what is being talked about.

(2) The critic can deny the doctrine that formally different utterances always differ in meaning, as I. A. Richards goes near to doing in *Interpretation in Teaching*. This may need some ingenious casuistry, but it is possible to establish the position sufficiently for literary purposes.

(3) The critic may accept this doctrine, and agree that difference of form is always difference of meaning. But he can still deny that the concept of style has disappeared. It has not disappeared; it has become subsumed in meaning. Style is a part of meaning, but a part which can properly and reasonably be discussed on its own.

For myself I should prefer the third of these possibilities—that style is an aspect of meaning; but I should expect to find literary critics employing all three, if not indiscriminately at least on different occasions and for different purposes. I shall not attempt to decide between these three positions—any one of them gives the critic all the room he needs to work in. What is now necessary is to show in practical and literary terms what aspects of the literary work it is intended to discuss under the head of style.

Whatever view we may take of its nature, it is clear that in talking about style we are talking about *choice*—choice between the varied lexical and syntactic resources of a particular language. And this is a secondary choice, a choice of means. In discussing whatever it is we mean by style we assume that the primary choice, the choice of subject-matter in the large sense, has already been made. The decision to write about the Trojan War, or whale-fishing, or a country childhood is not a stylistic one. We can talk about the secondary choice, the stylistic one, in various ways. We can say that it is the choice of the best verbal means to express a pre-determined subject-matter; or if we decline to do this we can talk about choice between the various meanings or shades of meaning that cluster round a given subject. (In practice it will be found to make surprisingly little difference which way we set about it.) We can regard the choice as conditioned by the subject-matter and the occasion, or as conditioned, perhaps unconsciously, by the character and temperament of the author. But whatever point of view we adopt, it will be the verbal ordonnance that we discuss, not the outlines of the myth, the facts of the case, the ideological or biographical substructure.

Let us begin by taking a simple case—virtually a non-literary one—the case of a scientific paper reporting the results of an experiment. It has several points of interest for our purpose. In the first place it could surely be maintained with some plausibility that there is here a pre-linguistic matter to be clothed in verbal dress. It would be possible not to write the paper at all, but simply to summon those with whom it was desired to communicate to witness a wordless repetition of the experiment. Or the result could be expressed entirely in mathematical formulae. If ever it is reasonable to talk about language as the dress of some pre-verbal complex of thought, surely it is here. But the strictly stylistic problem is limited; the range of choice is extremely narrow. Feeling is excluded in a scientific paper; tone (attitude towards the reader) is neutral; verbal play is superfluous or taboo. Yet even within these limits the stylistic choice still exists. It is possible to announce the subject of inquiry, to describe the experimental means used to investigate it, to state the results, in a variety of ways—economically or diffusely, clearly or obscurely. Above all it is possible to write the paper in such a way that curiosity is aroused, the resulting tension sustained for the appropriate time, the curiosity satisfied at the logically and psychologically appropriate points. And these things are all parts of what we will call style. It is possible that so much of style can occur even in a non-verbal medium—as when a mathematical paper is commended for its 'elegance'.

In a properly literary context the matter is always more complex and the possibilities of choice are far greater. The feeling of the writer towards his subject, his attitude towards the reader, both become significant. And here it is surely less appropriate to talk of a predetermined subject, which the writer can choose to express in one of a number of ways. The feeling and the tone are parts of what is to be expressed. They are parts of the meaning, not supererogatory embellishments or means of ingratiation. But however we choose to look at them, they are there to be discussed, and the verbal means by which such attitudes are established are open to observation. The choice of this word rather than that, of this kind of syntactical construction rather than another, is a visible fact, whose nature and effects can be examined. The initial response to a work of literature is general; we respond to the whole complex, without being aware of what goes to make it up. Most readers stop there, and feel no impulse to go farther. The minority whose interests lead them to closer inquiry may take a variety of courses. They may be led back from the work to its genesis in the author's experience; they may examine

the philosophic or religious ideas that it embodies; they
may concern themselves about its moral or social effects.
But if their interest is in the maker's art itself, rather
than in its causes or its effects, they will inquire into the
particular verbal means by which the total form has been
achieved. In that case the inquiry will be a stylistic one.
If its results bring about a new understanding of the
total literary form, the stylistic inquiry will have had real
critical results.

The organic unity of a work of literature is not something ready-made; it is not an entire and perfect chrysolite
found lying about in nature; it is something achieved.
This organic whole may be arrived at in a variety of
ways. The lyric poet sometimes has a rhythm in his
head before he knows what words will ever be found
to fit it; he may conceive a line or a phrase before he
knows what poem it is going to belong to; only on rare
occasions does he experience a whole poem as given,
dictated at once in its final shape. The expository writer
begins with an argument, perhaps vaguely apprehended
as a general form, but refined and knit together only in
the process of working out the appropriate organization,
syntax and vocabulary. The novelist can be aware of
fictional characters and situations, just as he can be
aware of characters and situations in life, without any
thought of their linguistic presentation. Most writing involves a process of revision, conducted either on paper
or in the mind before anything is written down. There is
some evidence that different writers look on this revising
process in very different lights; some see it as the pro-
gressively more accurate embodiment of a preconceived
meaning; some see it as a continual change and modification of meaning itself. In either case it is best for the
critic to look at the matter prospectively. The work of
literature is a project; when it is complete the result is a

unity, a whole. But it is a whole composed of linguistic elements that we also know in other combinations; we can therefore by a process of abstraction become aware of them separately and discuss them as contributions to the whole. The word that is magical in a particular line of poetry may be quite inert in a different sentence; the construction that is merely a bungle in one context may serve a powerful expressive purpose in another. It is with these phenomena, whatever our philosophy of meaning, whatever our theory about the psychology of the creative process, that the study of style is concerned.

The Beginnings of Modern Style-study

The effective impulses to modern style-study were various, but they can probably be reduced to two. One comes from historical linguistics and one from literary criticism. The impulse from criticism was largely an Anglo-American affair, that from linguistics was largely continental European, arising particularly out of Romance philology. The two still remain imperfectly united. Their aims were partly different, and there is no point in trying to reconcile studies that have different aims. However, in their most interesting work the two schools are really concerned with the same things, and it should be possible to see them both in the same perspective. In both cases the motive force was a reaction against scholastic disciplines that seemed mechanistic and external, hardly related at all to the living texture of literature. The European situation is described in a vivid passage of autobiography by the great Romance philologist Leo Spitzer:

When I attended the classes of French linguistics of my great teacher Meyer-Lübke no picture was offered us of the French people, or of the Frenchness of their language: in these classes we saw Latin *a* moving, according to relentless phonetic laws, toward French *e* (*pater, père*); there we saw a new system of declensions springing up from nothingness, a system in which the six Latin cases came to be reduced to two, and later to one. ... I was a long while realizing that Meyer-Lübke was offering only the *pre*history of French (as he established it by a comparison with the other Romance languages), not its history. And we were never allowed to contemplate a phenomenon in its quiet being, to look into its face : we always looked at its neighbours or at its predecessors.

When I changed over to the classes of the equally great literary historian Philipp August Becker, that ideal Frenchman seemed to show some faint signs of life—in the spirited analyses of the events in the *Pèlerinage de Charlemagne,* or of a Molière comedy; but it was as if the treatment of the contents were only subsidiary to the really scholarly work, which consisted in fixing the dates and historical data of these works of art, in assessing the amount of autobiographical elements and written sources which the poets had supposedly incorporated into their artistic productions (*Linguistics and Literary History*, 2).

It was from a dissatisfaction with this state of affairs that Spitzer came to evolve his own methods of style-study, designed to achieve a far more intimate and inward contact with the work of literary art. The passage above was written in 1948, of a period forty years earlier; and the discontents it is describing mark a movement in literary studies, paralleled, of course, in many other fields, away from the positivist methods of the nineteenth century. Spitzer combined in an unusual degree the equipment of the professional linguist with the tastes of an ardent and enthusiastic student of literature. Other European linguists approached the matter from a less

literary point of view. Charles Bally, for example, conceived of stylistics as the study of the expressive resources of a given language, and excluded from it the
study of literary language, language organized for an
aesthetic purpose. This self-denying ordinance was not
to be maintained, and Bally's followers, Cressot,
Marouzeau and Devoto, interested themselves also in the
literary manifestations of language. It remains true, however, that Continental style-study was conducted by
students of language rather than by men of letters in the
wider sense; and this has continued to affect the general
orientation of the subject.

In England the technical study of language was not
on the whole so highly developed, but the situation was
not greatly different from that described by Spitzer.
Literary studies at the beginning of this century were
largely dominated by Germanic philology; and much time
and energy was devoted to the linguistic study of Old
and Middle English. But the procedure remained arrested
at the Meyer-Lübke stage; it was very little extended
towards literary study and not at all towards more
modern literature. Literary studies were largely a matter
of literary history and annotation—facts about literature
rather than literature itself. What Spitzer says of Becker's
lectures was largely true of most literary study in the
Anglo-American sphere before the First World War; and if
these restrictions were evaded it was mainly by a way-
ward and unfocused belles-lettres.

It so happened that just about this time, in the years
preceding 1914, a new literary movement made its appearance. The poetry and criticism of T. S. Eliot, the
poetry and propaganda of Ezra Pound, the prose of
Joyce and the polemics of Wyndham Lewis were at
first a sort of underground movement in opposition to the
literary establishment; but they soon became something

like a literary establishment themselves. While doing many other things as well, these writers all tended, in their several ways, to focus attention on the verbal texture of the work of art, on literary craftsmanship, and to cast off as an obsolete irrelevance most of the external literary history and conventional literary judgment that had preceded them. This new critical outlook was at first quite divorced from the academies and from scholastic literary studies; but in a surprisingly short time it captured them, or was captured by them. No one lectured any more about the middle period of the novel of passion or the effect of the French Revolution on Wordsworth and Coleridge. The interest was in the texture of the poets' language, seen as a symptom of the quality of their imagination, a way into the heart of the creative process. In this way a strong impulse towards what can be called in the broadest sense style-study came from a totally new direction.

The literary history of this period is not my concern now, but a few illustrations should be offered. If we compare the immensely influential criticism of Eliot with that of, say, Arnold, we are at once struck by Eliot's much freer use of quotation. The argument is supported by close reference to particular passages. The prolonged elucidation of the nature of poetical wit in the essays on Marvell, the Metaphysical poets and Dryden is mainly developed by showing what is going on internally in particular poems and particular stanzas, and by contrasting these passages with others by poets of a different period. Wyndham Lewis opens his *Men without Art*, a book which develops into a piece of savage literary buccaneering, by contrasting a passage from Henry James with a greatly inferior passage from Aldous Huxley. The critics were hardly interested in detached scholarship; they were writing polemic and propaganda for their own literary movement. But as a by-product they were focusing attention on the intrinsic and interior constituents of the work of art, and so, in a way not at all to be expected, reveal some community of intention with a brilliant, purely academic scholar, such as Leo Spitzer.

The injection of these new literary ideas into academic study occurred at Cambridge in the 1920's. The real distinction of the Cambridge English school in its earlier and more challenging days was that it was the only university department in the world that knew anything about modern literature. It may be said that even Cambridge did not know much; but that would be an illegitimate hindsight. It was remarkable at the time we are discussing to find any awareness of modern literature and its new critical orientations in an academic setting. (*Experto crede:* in my own early education I saw something of what was happening on both sides of the fence.) I. A. Richards in his early teaching and writing called attention to Eliot's poetry and criticism; Eliot reviewed Richards's *Science and Poetry* in *The Dial*. The interchange thus begun was continued by F. R. Leavis. A brilliant, erratic Cambridge teacher, Mansfield Forbes, who left hardly any published work, was influential in two ways. His own lectures and classes offered examples of minute and sensitive internal analysis of poetry; and his effect on the development of Richards's work was very great. Richards came to literary studies from experimental psychology, and the application of his thinking to literature was enormously assisted by Forbes.

Richards, with his interest in semantics and communication theory, was deeply dissatisfied with the standards of reading and comprehension achieved by conventional literary training. The experiment recorded in his *Practical Criticism* was a piece of field-work designed to investigate this state of affairs. Short poems of varying degrees of complexity and merit were given to a mixed class of students and dons, without any indication of authorship or date, and they were asked to comment on them. The results revealed that without the aid of external information, literary history and the traditional judgments it brings in its train, a surprising number of educated readers were bewildered and helpless in interpreting what was before them. In the second part of the book Richards drew some theoretical conclusions from his experiment, and made a number of extremely valuable suggestions for improving matters. It is hardly too much to say that he provided a new apparatus for reading and interpreting literary texts. It was of course to a large extent a formalization of what the skilful reader had always done intuitively; but the fact remains that the method had never been made explicitly and generally accessible before.

The effects of this work were rapid and far-reaching. Something like an educational revolution in the teaching of literature took place in the thirties. The weight was taken off literary history, facts *about* literature, and attention was more and more concentrated on close reading and interpretation of individual works. Practical criticism, originally devised as a technique of inquiry, came to be used as an educational method, as it still is. Generations of literary students have been brought up to write, not historical essays, but analyses and interpretations of the works themselves, with close attention to verbal texture and organization. Richard's most brilliant pupil William Empson interested himself in the question of 'ambiguity', or the plurality of meaning in any highly organized piece of writing. The whole movement soon spread to the United States, where it formed the basis of what was there called the New Criticism, exemplified in the work of John Crowe Ransom, Cleanth Brooks and many others. The feed-back from this academic work to general criticism became evident before long. Un-supported judgments, mere statements of taste and pre-ference, were felt to be inadmissible; they had to be backed up by precise reference and analysis; and criti-cism, which by now meant largely stylistic criticism, began to make a claim for itself as an independent discipline.

This did not take place without a good deal of con-troversy, and the battle was long ago fought to the point of exhaustion. It is now obvious enough that positions tended to harden in a slightly absurd fashion; and the change in method, for all its indubitable bene-fits, began to reveal some attendant disadvantages. A false dichotomy between 'scholarly' and 'critical' studies grew up, and the new kind of stylistic criticism developed a somewhat cavalier attitude towards both historical and linguistic considerations. Gerard Manley Hopkins's phrase, 'low-latched in leaf-light housel', was gaily glossed by saying that it gained its concrete force from the word 'housel', which originally meant 'little house'. It never did, of course, mean anything of the sort, being derived from a Germanic root which means 'sacrifice' or 'holy thing'. The current meaning, in fact, is the same as the etymological one. Ingenious psychological explanations of metaphors and images were given when straightforward historical ones were staring us in the face. Most of these matters were arguable, and some of them are still argued about. What I believe is now evident is that this whole school of Anglo-American stylistic analysis, lively and invigorating as it often was, was also an extremely un-disciplined affair, and strangely innocent of scholarship. It was not based on any positive body of knowledge. In effect it disdained the appeal to knowledge of any kind, and rejoiced in being an intuitive free-for-all. To be im-partially disrespectful to both sides, we may say that if the vice of the Continental stylistics was pedantry, that of the Anglo-American school was irresponsibility.

In English and American scholarship 'practical criticism', 'explication', 'close reading', or whatever we like to call it, has developed into a convention without acquiring much more in the way of principles than it had to start with. It is now a convention less deadening than the external literary history that it replaced, but not much less. Yet no one can doubt that its gains were real. The intelligent student today has far better means of coming to grips with a work of literature in its own essence than any that were available fifty years ago. It seems likely that what is needed now is an injection of some real linguistic knowledge. It is not likely that the stylistic study of literature will ever become a science, but there is no need for it to be a riot of subjective fancy. Professional linguists are apt to say that their science has literary bearings to which students of literature pay insufficient attention. I think it is obvious that *most* of what the science of linguistics now does cannot be usefully related to literature at all; but there are bridges to be built, and it is in the area of stylistics that the opportunities for doing this are greatest. In the chapters that follow we shall examine what has been done in this field, and if possible see how different lines of a study could be brought together.

2

Linguistic style-study

Up to Saussure

As soon as we look at it at all closely, the difference between the literary and the linguistic study of style becomes evident. Charles Bally points out that until the nineteenth century language was never studied for its own sake. It was always a question of what advantage could be derived from linguistic study—for the logical formulation of thought, for correctness of style, above all for the understanding of the classical writers, regarded not only as literary models but as linguistic norms. This brought a number of consequences in its train: a reverence for the written language; a corresponding devaluation of the spoken language, which was regarded as vulgar; the superstition of an unchangeable classic language, proper as a model for all time, which should be guarded against all innovation by a jealous purism. The innovations, of course, occurred; the forms of purism changed from age to age, and the situation was complicated by the fact that the ultimately unchallengeable standards were situated in the dead languages, not in the living vernaculars. The idea of a stylistic standard fixed in the past or in another country is deeply rooted in our culture. Horace in the *Ars Poetica* refers the Latin writers to Greek models. The prestige of Ciceronian Latin was so high in the Renaissance that it became the obvious duty of the modern prose writer simply to imitate it. True, there were rebellions. Politian defiantly asserted, *'Non Ciceronem me tamen exprimo'*—I am not expressing Cicero but myself. This did not, however, prevent generations of schoolboys for 300 years after Politian's time being assiduously trained in the pastiche of Latin prose and Greek verses. When in seventeenth-century England a new generation revolted against the elaborate periodic syntax and the formal decorative rhythms of Ciceronian prose, the alternative first arrived was not to write as one spoke or as the occasion demanded, but simply to switch to another classic model—Seneca instead of Cicero. And 100 years later we find Swift believing that the English language, having reached its stage of classical perfection, should be fixed in that state, and all future deviations should be prevented.

It must I think be admitted that this has been the normal literary attitude to problems of language for most of our history. In this as in other matters the watershed is the nineteenth century. It is then that the scientific study of language begins, and it participates in the historical and evolutionary attitude that pervades all nineteenth-century thought. A century that saw the rise of evolutionary biology, anthropology and modern historiography was not likely to remain attached to the idea of an immutable linguistic norm fixed somewhere in the distant past. The first great development was that of comparative philology, in practice the comparative study of the Indo-European languages. The discovery of Sanskrit and the observation that it had affinities with the modern European languages was made by the Orientalist William Jones (d. 1794); but the systematic organization of these facts dates from 1816 when Franz

Bopp published his work on the conjugation of Sanskrit, which studies the relation of Sanskrit with Latin, Greek and the Germanic tongues. This was the beginning of a linguistic science that continued to develop throughout the century. The great popularizer of these researches in England was Max Müller (*Lessons on the Science of Languages*, 1861). Determinedly evolutionary in its methods, formed on a biological model (languages are arranged in 'families', words have 'roots'), comparative philology traced the development of verbal and grammatical forms through time and space, from the reconstructed 'primitive Aryan' to the vernaculars of today. It is a late stage of these studies that Spitzer describes in his account of the lectures of Meyer-Lübke; and he puts his finger very precisely on their limitations. Isolated linguistic forms were studied in their development through time (*diachronically*, to use a later terminology): but the whole state of a language at a given time was never presented for inspection. Still less did comparative philology, boring its deep and narrow tunnels into the past, provide any apparatus for studying the actual state of the language in the living present.

The great change, the second great development of modern linguistics, came with Ferdinand de Saussure. The work of Saussure published during his lifetime reveals him as a distinguished comparative philologist of the old school. His first important publication was a treatise on the vowel system of the Indo-European languages (1879), and he continued to labour in the same field. But between 1906 and 1911 he gave three courses in general linguistics which so changed their objectives as to constitute a veritable new departure in the study of language. He never published these lectures, and it turned out after his death that they had never been systematically written down at all. They had, however, made such a deep im-

c

pression of originality that a group of his pupils took on the difficult and laborious task of reconstructing them from his own notes. The result was the celebrated *Cours de linguistique générale*, published in 1915, from which most modern linguistics is considered to take its origin.

The main point in Saussure's work, and also the one of most interest for our purpose, is that he makes an absolute disjunction between *diachronic* and *synchronic* linguistics. Diachronic linguistics is historical linguistics —in effect, the old comparative philology that we have briefly described. By synchronic linguistics is meant the study of the actual state of a language at a given time, conceived as a complete, interdependent system of communication, actualized in daily life and divorced entirely from its history and origins. It is this kind of linguistic study that Saussure succeeds in getting on its feet. It is the study of language as a present and living organism, as against the study of its fossil remains. When Browning's Renaissance grammarian 'Gave us the doctrine of the enclitic δε,/Dead from the waist down', the death of his members is a symbol of Browning's own almost prophetic feeling about the deadness of such studies; and 'The Grammarian's Funeral' joins hands with Spitzer's account of Meyer-Lübke's lectures. It was Saussure's work that brought linguistics into relation with the living language; and, quite unliterary as it was, this could hardly fail in the end to have some influence on literary studies.

The second point in Saussure's course was the distinction between *la langue* and *la parole*. *La langue* for Saussure is a definite element abstracted from the heterogeneous facts of language in general. It is the public, conventional aspect of language, the system established by a sort of social contract among the members of a community which alone makes it possible for them to understand each other. It is *la langue* that is described in dictionaries and grammars; and they are only possible because *la langue* exists, necessary and unalterable by individual volition. For *la langue* is always external to the individual; he inherits it, he is born into it as he is born into a society; it is not a function of his individual will. *La parole*, on the other hand, is individual utterance, an act of will and intelligence, serving individual ends. *La langue* is a code, and *la parole* is the way the code is used in an actual situation, or the ways in which it is habitually used by an individual speaker. It is only in *la parole* that *la langue* is actualized; yet *la parole* would be impossible without the public, social system of *la langue*. The linguistics of *la parole* were not much discussed by Saussure and were considerably more developed by his pupil, Bally. But the mere distinction is important for stylistics; it contains the germ of the idea, so often appearing in discussions of style, that there is an impersonal norm of which style is the specialized or individual variant.

Bally and His Successors

Saussure is not much interested in the literary manifestations of language. For him the primary object of the linguist's study is what he calls the 'natural' sphere of language—the spoken language. The written language, the literary language, the language of poetry are specializations, more or less detached from this living reality. These ideas were carried much further by Bally, and he is no more inclined than his master to move in the direction of literature. Bally is virtually the inventor of the term 'Stylistics' but he does not mean by it the study of literary style. At the base of Bally's thought is the idea of language in the service of life, language as a function of life, soaked in human affections, mingled with human strivings, existing only to fulfil the purposes of life itself. Language so conceived is the only real and living language that exists. Everything else is an abstraction made for purposes of study, or a specialized use, belonging to a particular activity or a particular *milieu*. Current colloquial speech is as worthy of study as the most refined literary utterance—for the linguist indeed more worthy of study.

The natural language, such as we all speak, is neither in the service of pure reason nor of art; it does not have in view either a logical or a literary ideal; its primary and constant function is not to construct syllogisms, to round off periods, to conform itself to the laws of the alexandrine. It is simply in the service of life, not the life of a few, but of all, and in all its manifestations; its function is biological and social (*Le langage et la vie*, 14).

What then is stylistics? We associate the word with a more or less literary inquiry; but for Bally it is the study of expressive effects and mechanisms in all language—*la langue de tout le monde*. The conception depends entirely on a distinction between the 'logical' and the 'affective' characters of language. The 'logical' aspect of language, the expression of pure ideas, the communication of facts in themselves, is an abstraction, realized only in the artificial language of science, and then imperfectly. *Aucun homme ne vit par la seule intelligence; il n'y a pas d'idée pure qui aide à vivre.* My 'lived' thought is of quite another material than pure ideas; actual language is everywhere penetrated with strivings, affections, judgments of feeling and judgments of value. The intellectual judgment *The earth turns* changes into a judgment of value in the mouth of Galileo crying before his judges: '*E pur si muove!*' Saussure's linguistics had concentrated chiefly on the impersonal system, *la langue.* Bally's stylistics studies all the ways in which this impersonal system is converted into the stuff of living human utterance.

His method is to consider all these living characters of language as deviations from a norm. At first Bally used the word 'affective' to describe such deviations, but this proved too narrow, and later he talks of 'affective and expressive' characteristics. The first norm proposed is 'the logical or intellectual mode of expression, which one might also call the language of the abstract, or the language of pure ideas'. It is against this that the affective characters of language are measured; the plain formulation serves as the standard, against which is set the formulation coloured by interest, feeling, pleasure or displeasure, approval or disapproval. But there is another class of particularities that require notice. These are not primarily affective, but social. Certain modes of expression suggest a certain social *milieu*—popular, refined, learned, provincial or what not. Bally calls such effects *faits d'évocation*; and these evocative effects are only possible because there is also a norm against which they are set—the common language, uncoloured by any special social suggestions. Among these special dialects evocative of a *milieu* Bally includes the written language, the literary language, scientific language and familiar language. The total result of such investigations applied to a single linguistic communitity is to provide a description of the entire expressive resources of the language as a whole. Bally's *Traité de stylistique française* does this for French; Marouzeau's *Traité de stylistique appliqué au latin* does the same for Latin. It is this study of the whole expressive equipment of a language that is Bally's principal aim.

It is obvious that there is a great deal here that is of the highest interest to the student of literature. As soon as he turns his attention to the texture and detail of literary utterance it is precisely with such transformations that he is concerned. Yet as a linguist Bally expressly refuses to make this transition:

There is an impassable gulf between the use of language by an individual in the common, general circumstances imposed on a whole linguistic group, and the use made of it by a poet, a novelist, an orator. When the speaker is placed in the same conditions as all other members of the group, there exists by reason of this very fact a norm by which one can measure the deviations of individual expression: for the *littérateur* the conditions are quite different; he makes a *voluntary and conscious use of language* ... secondly, and above all, *he uses language with an aesthetic intention*; he strives to create beauty with words, as a painter does with colours or a musician with sounds (*Traité de stylistique française*, 19).

But surely this can be questioned. Bally may personally refuse to extend his consideration to literature; but it does not seem nearly as certain as he supposes that such an extension cannot be made. His contrast between the spontaneous utterance of common life and the conscious, voluntary utterance of literary composition is by no means absolute. Some speakers choose their words with care; some literary men write with great spontaneity and freedom. His argument that aesthetic intention introduces an entirely new dimension into language, removing it from all ordinary considerations, is more formidable. A measure of discontinuity is real enough. All literature exists within, as it were, a parenthesis, distinguishing it from actual discourse. But within the parenthesis all the effects that have been observed outside it are still active. Affective qualities, qualities evocative of a *milieu*, occur in literature as much as they do in common speech. It seems therefore that Bally's limitation is unnecessary. The precise and detailed observation of semantic and syntactical features that he applies to common speech could equally be applied to literature, and the analysis of literary works might well benefit from it.

Some of Bally's disciples indeed refuse to follow him at this point. Marcel Cressot (*Le style et ses techniques*, 1947) expressly makes this dissociation:

In agreement with M. Bally up to now, we are going to part company with him. . . . For us the literary work is simply a communication, and all the aesthetics that the writer puts into it are no more than the means of securing the reader's attention more firmly. This concern is perhaps more systematic than in current communication, but it is not of a different kind. We would even say the work of literature is *par excellence* the domain of stylistics, precisely because there the choice is more 'voluntary' and more 'conscious' (p. 3).

But although Cressot here takes a step into what Bally regarded as an impassable gulf, although he makes use of and discusses literary examples, he does not proceed very far into the territory of the man of letters. He analyses literary devices, but makes no attempt at the analysis of a work of art. When all is said, the work of this school belongs to linguistics rather than to literature. What literary studies could learn from it is a technique of accurate linguistic observation, a descriptive apparatus with some pretensions to completeness. If Anglo-American 'practical criticism' had had any such foundations we should have seen less of the merely capricious, less pursuit of mere fortuitous crotchets, fewer attempts to explain all literary phenomena by the use of some fashionable catchword. Bally talks of stylistics as a science; and literary style-study is never likely to be that. But the attempt to give it some sort of scientific foundation, some basis of ordered and demonstrable knowledge, might have made it a less chancy and arbitrary affair than it has been.

3

Literary stylistics:
methods and problems

Stylistics and Literary Art

The field of literary stylistics is so wide that no attempt
can be made here to give a systematic record of its
evolution, especially as the developments have occurred
in several countries—parallel, overlapping or correlated.
In the next chapter I shall give some account of the
work of outstanding practitioners; in this one I shall out-
line the topics and problems that literary stylistics attempts to deal with.

A marked contrast can be seen between the rigorous
and restricted methods of the Bally school of stylistics
and the relatively expansive procedure of those who were
more concerned with literature as an art. Bally and his
followers were concerned with establishing a general system of stylistic possibilities that could be applied to all
literary work as it could be applied to all types of utterance. A keystone of their system was the setting up of a
norm against which stylistic deviations could be measured.
From the literary point of view it is open to question
chiefly for taking uncoloured descriptive language as the
paradigm of all language. This may be a legitimate
methodological convenience, but there seems a certain
perversity in it, since on Bally's own showing 'natural'

language is hardly ever of this kind. The contrast can be seen in the work of certain Germanic writers whose primary point of reference is not a norm or a method but the total being of a work of literary art. The difficulty here is to distinguish anything that can be specifically called 'stylistics'. How does *Stilforschung* so conceived differ from the vast unorganized field of literary criticism —criticism of the ordinary historical, impressionistic or belletristic kinds, which stylistics was supposed to improve on?

This can be illustrated in the work of Karl Vossler, a writer of enormous and various learning. His vast work on Dante (*Die Göttliche Komodie*, Heidelberg, 1907-10) is mainly a profound and detailed inquiry into all the various streams of medieval culture that contributed to Dante's thought. The American translation of the book is simply called *Medieval Culture*, and this suggests what is indeed the case, that the bulk of the work is cultural history, not style-study at all. The long chapter on 'The Poetry of the *Divine Comedy*' is an attempt to give a stylistic analysis of the whole poem. But an attempt on such a huge scale almost necessarily misses the specificity and refinement that stylistic analysis demands. There is nothing distinctive in the method, which indeed boils down to a rehearsal of the incidents of the *Commedia*, and a commentary on their emotional force, order and arrangement—traditional literary commentary of a rather pedestrian kind. Vossler seems to have been obsessed with the *idea* of the internal analysis of a literary work, without ever being able to decide on its precise bearing and purpose. His book on Benvenuto Cellini is in essence a psychological study; and in other works Vossler is attracted to the study of national characteristics as expressed through literary style (*The Spirit of Language* is too much preoccupied with the German soul to be congenial to non-Teutonic readers). Vossler's conclusion, shared also by others, is that style-analysis simply coincides with literary criticism in its 'objective' form. It is simply literary criticism with the element of arbitrary personal preference purged away.

Another way of defining stylistics is found in Hatzfeld's clumsily titled essay, 'Stylistic Criticism as Art-minded Philology'. The distinction is indeed indicated in the title: stylistic analysis is simply philology in the traditional German sense (i.e. literary and linguistic study), with the aesthetic dimension added. Bally's stylistics, equally with Meyer-Lübke's comparative philology, severely renounced aesthetic considerations. If all or any of these lines of investigation are re-directed towards aesthetic objects we have literary stylistics. But these methodological considerations soon become extremely arid; let us elucidate the situation a little farther by thinking of the actual topics which literary stylistics has investigated.

Special Expressive Devices

Nearest to the methods of Bally and his school is the study of particular expressive devices. In the work of Cressot, Marouzeau and the linguists this occurs simply as a part of a general stylistic organon, the total stylistic tool-kit of a given language. Alter the context, study a particular stylistic device as it is employed in an individual work of art, or the work of an individual writer, and we are at once within the literary sphere. We are inquiring how a specific configuration of language is used for a specific aesthetic purpose, or by what linguistic means a particular aesthetic purpose is achieved. Studies of special kinds of imagery, special choices of vocabulary, special syntactical usages, all come under this head. I shall not attempt to cover the extent and variety of this kind of work. For that, as for all other kinds of study referred to in this chapter, the reader must be referred to Hatzfeld's valuable *Bibliography of the New Stylistics*, for the Romance languages; and the recently published *English Stylistics: a Bibliography*, by Bailey and Burton. Among the mass of bibliographical material on individual authors and periods the distinctive existence of stylistic work is not easily recognized. Let us take as illustration the study of one particular stylistic procedure—the so-called *style indirect libre*.

The ordinary grammatical distinction between direct and indirect speech is known to everyone. It was in the novel that the existence of another form was observed, a form in which the context, the containing structure, is that of indirect or reported speech, while a number of elements (syntactic and lexical) of direct speech are also allowed to remain. To the ordinary literary student this may seem a trivial observation, but in the work of a number of novelists it turns out to be a persistently employed procedure, with its own distinctive flavour. It is frequent in Jane Austen:

Scarcely had they passed the sweep-gate and joined the other carriage, than she found her subject cut up—her hand seized, her attention demanded, and Mr. Elton actually making violent love to her: *availing himself of the precious opportunity, declaring sentiments which must be already well known, hoping—fearing—ready to die if she refused him; but flattering himself that his ardent attachment and unequalled love and unexampled passion could not fail of having some effect*, and, in short very much resolved on being seriously accepted as soon as possible (*Emma*, Chapter 15).

Here the presentation is formally that of objective narrative, narrative presented as fact; but the parts printed in italics diverge from this—they are a paraphrased version of what Mr. Elton actually said; the expression with its absurdities and conventionalities is neither Jane Austen's nor Emma's, but Mr. Elton's. Syntactically, however, it is assimilated to the narrative: 'She found Mr. Elton availing himself of the precious opportunity, declaring sentiments', etc. It could quite easily have been presented in direct speech: ' "I avail myself of the precious opportunity," said Mr. Elton, "my sentiments must already be well known to you. I flatter myself that my ardent attachment cannot fail of having some effect." ' In other places Jane Austen does present such incidents in this way. On the other hand, it could all have been done as objective narrative: 'She found Mr. Elton actually making violent love to her', etc., and the passage could have been continued in the uncoloured objective manner. What we actually have is an intermediate form.

The existence of this form was first remarked in an article by Bally in 1912, and, following his usual programme, he studied it simply as a current linguistic device. Eight years later Proust, in an article in the *Nouvelle Revue Française*, remarked on Flaubert's use of this device, quite unconscious that it had been noticed before. A. Thibaudet replied to him in a letter: two years later he brought out his study of Flaubert, and in the admirable chapter on Flaubert's style the discussion of this particular effect occupies a prominent place. From then on a voluminous literature on the subject has grown up (see R. Ullmann's *Style in the French Novel*, 94–8). The form has been traced back as far as La Fontaine, becomes more prominent in the late eighteenth century, and almost a standard practice in nineteenth-century fiction, alike in French, English and German.

Much of the discussion of this device has been a technical analysis of its various syntactic manifestations. Some of these are trivial, but the method as a whole clearly has literary significance. It is obviously connected with the tendency to reduce the role of the omnicompetent narrator, to incorporate the point of view of the characters into the structure of the narrative. It is a part, therefore, of a general movement in fiction from the early nineteenth century on. It may be variously motivated. It may spring from the desire to *present* rather than merely to *tell about* the incidents of the story. It may be a means of bringing in the subjectivity of the characters, of portraying their inner life, while preserving a greater measure of authorial control than could be done by the use of simple direct speech. This is often the case with Flaubert. It may be there simply to give a flavour of liveliness and colour to passages of merely functional narrative:

For half an hour Mr. Weston was surprised and sorry; but then he began to perceive that Frank's coming two or three months later would be a much better plan, *better time of year, better weather*; and that he would be able; without any doubt, to stay considerably longer with them than if he had come sooner (*Emma*, Chapter 18).

Here the words italicized, with their abrupt, cheerful, colloquial tone are obviously Mr. Weston's; and they are introduced much as a lively speaker will slip half-unconsciously into mimicry in recounting the actions and conversation of others. Perhaps more important than any of these, the free indirect style, with its close collocation of the author's point of view and that of his characters, becomes the vehicle of irony. It is therefore one of the most important means by which the author can convey his judgments and valuations without obviously intrusive commentary. The examination of

Flaubert's methods (by Proust, Thibaudet and Ullmann, among others) has shown that the device has become an integral part of the fabric of his prose, a procedure by which some of his most characteristic effects are obtained. An inspection of Jane Austen's methods has persuaded me that the same is true of her. And none of this can be demonstrated without the detailed examination of verbal technique that we call 'stylistics'.

Still within the field of the novel, a more extended kind of investigation is the study of narrative method in general—first person as against third person; direct narration by an 'omniscient' author, or the use of the point of view of the internal characters; interior monologue, 'stream of consciousness' methods; and so on. The impulse to these inquiries was largely given by the prefaces of Henry James, and a recent example is Wayne Booth's admirable and comprehensive study, *The Rhetoric of Fiction*. In poetry the tendency has been more towards the study of individual authors; but the isolation of such qualities as 'wit' and 'irony' which has played such a large part in recent poetical criticism is also an investigation of particular stylistic devices. Again the split between 'stylistics' and general criticism can be observed. Formally stylistic studies attempt to be neutral and objective; in more general criticism the observation and analysis is often in the service of some other end. Since there are always conventional judgments to be re-examined, and since every age makes its special demands, this must always be so. But it should be one of the functions of stylistics in the narrower sense to give partial and tendentious criticism some solid material to work on.

Other stylistic devices that can be studied in similar ways are almost innumerable: word-order, repetition, rhythmical and musical patterns, metaphor, symbol and imagery, local colour, synaesthetic effects. Some of these are obviously of greater range and centrality than others: but it will commonly be found that almost any stylistic pecularity that is genuinely prominent and observable in a particular writer can serve as a key to his artistic procedure. Literary critics who are unaccustomed to stylistic analysis tend to be sceptical about the significance of such investigations. They often, indeed, look unpromising from the outside; it is only by actually using such studies. or, better still, making them oneself, that their value as a way into the work of literary art can be experienced. It must be added that many of these stylistic inquiries are designedly limited to observation, analysis and record. To the critic of a comprehensive turn of mind these give an impression of incompleteness. They become authentic literary studies only when the linguistic observation is *used*—when conclusions are drawn from it that tell us something of importance about the nature and meaning of the work as a whole.

Individual Style

The most familiar kind of style-study is the study of individual style of a single author. The Romantic emphasis on style as the expression of individual personality has brought this to the notice even of unliterary readers, and post-Romantic depreciation of the expressive outlook has put this particular approach somewhat under a cloud. But there is no need to cross the line from literary study to illicit biography, and in fact the study of individual style is universally practised on various levels of technical sophistication. A literary work is a verbal structure and even the critic who is primarily interested in the history of ideas or the social implications of literature can hardly proceed beyond generalities without paying some attention to the way in which words are used. It may again be asked therefore how style-study differs from general literary criticism. The broad answer is that in many kinds of criticism attention to verbal texture may be intermittent, often unaware of itself and often uncritical of its own methods. Many critics begin from biography, from literary history or the history of thought and arrive at close consideration of the literary work itself only at the end. The characteristic feature of style-study is that it begins from the literary work itself, from words and the way they are combined in a particular body of writing. There is no limit beyond which the student of style is forbidden to go, but at least he starts from a positive and identifiable point.

Whoever begins to look into these matters will immediately be struck by the immense body of such work in the Romance languages and their relative paucity in English. The tendency to separation between linguistic and literary studies in the English-speaking world has meant that comparatively few students of literature have been willing to begin from close consideration of language. Indeed, the consideration of a writer's language frequently comes as a sort of icing on the cake after every other aspect of his work has been dealt with. The claim of stylistics rests essentially on the proposition that the farthest ranges of a writer's art, the depths of his emotional experience, the heights of his spiritual insight, are expressed only through his words and can be apprehended only through an examination of his verbal art. Even if this claim is admitted it must also be admitted that there is a genuine difficulty in making the transition to these larger considerations from the particular features of vocabulary and syntax with which the style student generally starts, and that short-cuts of various kinds are possible. The equipment of the linguist is frequently

D

different from that of the literary student, the one being inclined to positive observation, the other to intuitive perception and speculation; and apart from temperamental differences of this kind there are real difficulties of method. We are most of us incurably inclined to think of ideas as the ultimate reality and words as their merely accidental clothing, and over large areas this view may have considerable justification. An expository writer working within a well-established convention may exhibit nothing particularly individual or characteristic in his way of handling words and may afford very little material for the student of style to work upon. And even when he is considering an imaginative writer the literary student may often find that he has had very little training in observing the correlation between an intuitively observed literary quality and the specific verbal means by which it has been brought about. It is precisely this kind of training that stylistic study professes to give. But it must be confessed that it was some time before style-study arrived at this point.

At one extreme we have the pure linguistic approach. This tends to work by accumulation, by a complete inventory of the stylistic qualities of an author – vocabulary, sentence structure, syntactic peculiarities, imagery and so forth, listed according to some predetermined scheme. In much early work of this kind no literary conclusions were drawn. What we have is virtually an accumulation of evidence on which such conclusions might be based, but no more. A further effect of this procedure is that in a complete inventory much of what is recorded may virtually be waste matter. Many of the qualities described have nothing particularly characteristic about them and lead to no increase of literary understanding. Much of what is presented is not the fruit of authentic observation but results rather from the mechanical

application of a set scheme. It is the prevalence of such
studies in which the aesthetic dimension has either been
renounced or has never been arrived at that has given
rise to a suspicion of stylistic work among many literary
students. Much will naturally depend on the nature of
the author under consideration. A pedestrian novelist
like Trollope may at first sight offer very little purchase
for a stylistic investigation. But it must be remembered
that his humour, his humanity, his understanding of the
society of his time, whatever qualities we find in him,
have only been materialized through verbal means and
they must in principle therefore be open to verbal investigation. In the case of an intricate and difficult author
like Mallarmé stylistic investigation is obviously required. His syntax needs elucidation in order that it may
be merely understood. His vocabulary is often thought
to be excessively rarefied and we need to know from
what sources it is drawn. It is often said that his style
has been deeply influenced by his study of English. But
the student will want to know whether this is really so;
whether English syntax really does anything to explain
the extraordinary behaviour of Mallarmé's sentences. All
these matters have been investigated in an admirable
study by J. Schèrer, which although it expressly re-
nounces all consideration of meaning, all consideration of
the total bearing and significance of Mallarmé's art, yet
succeeds in being an indispensable preliminary to any
wider understanding. And since in the case of Mallarmé
so much of his total significance is realized in his intricate
struggle with means of expression, even a study so de-
liberately limited as this one can be of great literary
significance.

At the other extreme from these linguistic procedures
we have literary criticism which deals with stylistic
matters in an entirely unsystematic way. Such criticism

is apt to ask questions without suggesting any plausible means of answering them, while on the other hand remaining unaware that there are real questions to which more or less verifiable answers can be found. At its best such criticism may achieve great intuitive insight or have programmatic value in changing the direction of literary ideas. T. S. Eliot's essays on Marvell, the Metaphysical poets, and Dryden are of this kind. At its worst, criticism of this type is a mere orgy of opinion. An example of the worst would be F. R. Leavis' celebrated essay on Milton's verse. That this curious paroxysm should for long have been accepted as a serious contribution to literature is an indication of how low the intellectual level of literary discussion in England could sink during the thirties and forties. Stylistic analysis must begin with an act of submission to the work as it is in itself. Leavis's essay begins from a prefabricated judgment—a second-hand judgment, since his conviction that Milton has been dislodged is merely a vulgarization of ideas that Eliot had already worked out in the essays mentioned above. The condemnation of Milton's style is unsupported by analysis or accurate description. Long quotations are offered, but nothing is done with them. The old school-master's dictum that Milton wrote English as though it were Latin is repeated, but no syntactical demonstration is offered. Otherwise the argument is sustained entirely by rhetoric. The norm of comparison suggested for Milton is Shakespeare—that is to say, an epic poet is compared with a dramatic poet; a poet who writes almost entirely of events and objects beyond this world is compared with a poet who writes almost entirely of events and objects on middle earth. If this is criticism, the distinction between it and stylistic analysis will be clear. However, this would be to reduce the idea of criticism to an absurdity. And it is only fair to add that there are many examples of critical description, which start from *parti-pris* or the desire to prove a point, as the stylistic analyst does not, but still make a genuine attempt at understanding: and some of these are by Leavis himself.

Effective style-study must lie somewhere between these two—between hard-line linguistics and subjective criticism. It is a dogma in much recent criticism that description involves evaluation, but this may be doubted. Accurate and evaluatively neutral criticism is neither impossible nor useless. Stylistic description almost inevitably depends on comparison with some norm and this norm should be seen to be a relevant one. The language of a novelist might quite properly be viewed in the light of the language of common life: but with an epic poet in the classical tradition there would be very little sense in talking in these terms. Style-study need not involve pedantry or a self-conscious excess of system. French critics in particular offer many brilliant examples of style-study conducted with that immense sense of responsibility towards language in which French critics are on the whole so much superior to the English, and conducted also with the elegance and lucidity of ordinary literary discourse, entirely without pedantry or technicality. The same thing may, of course, be done in a more scholastic and technical manner. The German writers in particular tend to be devotees of system and to write less for the general, educated reader. What all genuine literary style studies ought to have in common is that they are not mere catalogues of linguistic features, but are directed to the understanding of a work of art.

Such studies are likely to abandon the complete inventory and to be more selective in their methods. But how is the selection of stylistic features for examination initially made? There is always the danger of a mere arbitrary selection of features which happens to have struck a particular observer, for accidental or subjective reasons. This can often be avoided by putting the individual style-study in its historical setting. The individual utterance of a novelist is compared with the common speech or the general narrative style of his time. The individual utterance of a poet is brought into relief by seeing it as a divergence from the general practice of a school; as, for instance, when we compare the language of Gerard Manley Hopkins with that of the generality of Victorian poetry. Obviously if this is to yield useful results it is important to select the right frame of reference. But we can argue in quite another way; it can be said that any point of entry may serve as means of access to an author's work, and that any approach if carried far enough will lead to its centre. An extremely interesting essay by Sir George Rostrevor-Hamilton, 'The Tell-tale Article', arrives at some penetrating observations about modern English poets, simply by examining their use of the definite article. To discover what stylistic features will be revealing is largely a matter of experience and intuitive talent. We will reserve further consideration of this matter until we discuss the work of Leo Spitzer in the next chapter, since Spitzer has made this method his own.

It is relevant to ask what the object of an individual style-study ought to be. Much of the linguistic work we have discussed seems quite untroubled by these considerations; it seems to regard style-study as an end in itself, and to be quite content with a mere listing of an author's idiosyncrasies of expression. On this basis it is hardly possible to distinguish mere mannerisms from important expressive qualities, or trivial and accidental habits from profoundly important imaginative means of expression. Once we go beyond these limits, perhaps the most frequent and obvious aim of individual style-study has been psychological. If we want to see the mere bundle of expressive characteristics as part of a totality, the totality that seems most obviously to present itself is the personality of the author. The wild exuberance, the mock learning. the profuse verbal coinages of Rabelais; the marmoreal self-conscious coldness of Landor's style—these are easily seen as the expressions of a particular type of character; and correlations of this kind are not hard to make. Such studies may even become psychoanalytical, and they may very well end by taking us outside literature all together. But the naïve equation of what a writer reveals in his work with his historic personality is always very uncertain. The sculptural serenity of Landor's literary attitude seems to have been largely a defence against a passionate and disordered temperament. A much more legitimate and much more rewarding study occurs if we shift the terms a little—if we transfer our attention from the historic personality of a writer to his creative personality, to his imaginative function. It is not enough to regard style, metaphorically speaking, as the artist's personal handwriting, and to treat it as a graphologist would treat actual handwriting. The literary style-analyst is studying works of art, not varieties of human character. That these works are the outcome of a particular temperament may have a peripheral interest; but the real object of the student's search is the organizing aesthetic principle.

If the study is of a single work, or splits itself up into studies of single works, we fairly obviously replace psychology by an examination of the artefact itself. Most criticism begins by studying the major structure—plot or character, thought or feeling. Style-study begins as it were at the other end of the scale, with the precise verbal manifestations; and this is not only a manner of method; it enshrines a kind of faith—a faith that it is only by the close and intimate examination of verbal texture that the true being of a work of literary art can ever be reached. Movements in this direction can be seen everywhere in modern critical writing. Wilson Knight sees a Shakespearian play as an expanded metaphor; T. S. Eliot is apt to depreciate the originality and importance of the poet's thought and concentrate attention on his verbal medium. The logical end of this process should be a more exact attention to the verbal medium than informal and intuitive criticism can generally attain. It is this that style-analysis aims to supply.

The study of an individual style conceived in this way may broaden out from pure linguistic description to include almost anything found in general criticism. But there are some exclusions. An essay like Leavis's on Milton's verse is essentially polemical and tendentious in its intention. It does not aim at an accurate description of Milton's language and rhythms; it is sketchy, suggestive and highly coloured. Nor does it aim at penetrating with sympathy and understanding to the heart of Milton's poetry; its purpose is to change the direction of taste. Tendencies of this kind are quite common in criticism, though usually to a less extravagant degree. There are various reasons, some creditable, some less so, for which a critic may aim at the indoctrination of his readers rather than at the increase of understanding. The criticism of a poet is often disguised propaganda for his own creative work or for that of his friends; the criticism of a man deeply engaged in the literary controversies of the day is propaganda for a sect, a party or a school of thought. Stylistic analysis on the other hand aims at objectivity; some have even said that its purpose is a scientific knowledge of literature. All claims to turn literary study into a science are extremely dubious; it is hard to imagine a state of affairs in which the style-study of an individual author could arrive at the incontrovertible status of a scientific demonstration. There will always be room for disagreement about the distribution of emphasis, about the relative importance of different features observed; but it is possible to point out objectively the existence of certain linguistic features; it is possible to arrange these in a logically and psychologically compelling order; and it is possible to bind these together into an argument that can reach, if not certainty, at least a very high degree of persuasiveness. No one would wish to wipe out the partisan and speculative elements from criticism altogether, but there is a great deal to be said for founding them on a basis of agreed, demonstrable analysis and description.

Possibilities and limitations will be exhibited more fully in the next chapter, when we discuss the work of individual practitioners, but some illustrations may be given here. Dr. Johnson as a prose writer has a very strongly marked style, clearly differentiated from that of his immediate predecessors. An obvious way of beginning the study of his style would be to distinguish it from that of the age of Swift and Addison. Certain features of his sentence-structure, such as his continual use of antithesis, command immediate attention. When, however, we begin to inquire into the function, the purpose of this balanced and antithetical sentence-structure, we at once tread on less certain ground. To a superficial observer it would seem to correspond to something assured, commonsensical and logical in Johnson's mind; but a rather closer examination makes this seem less likely. Many of his antitheses turn out on inspection to be decorative rather than functional; they serve scarcely any logical purpose, they seem to be there rather because Johnson enjoyed them. From there we could go on to consider Johnson's theoretical views on prose composition, his belief that

the important truths are all known in advance and that
the function of the writer is chiefly to present the familiar
in a striking and effective manner. This accounts for some
of the features of his balanced and formal prose style
but not for all; there is a good deal left over that seems
to contain an element of sheer play, a delight in verbal
patterning for its own sake, a delight always kept in
check by a sober, responsible and morally oriented mind.
If we continued on these lines we should be moving
towards a description of the whole nature of Johnson's
creative impulse.

It would not, however, be very profitable on the whole
to consider Johnson's prose works as individual aesthetic
objects. Much of his work was occasional in its origin
and utilitarian in its purpose; almost all of it was part of
a continual process of musing, reflecting, informing,
moralizing rather than full imaginative creation. We
should be rather less inclined to discuss the style of, say,
a lyric poet in these wholesale and comprehensive terms,
for we expect the productions of the lyric poet each
to be a self-subsistent entity. If we were to take a major
lyrical reflective poem—say, Keats' 'Ode to a Nightingale'
or Wallace Stevens' 'Sunday Morning'—we should hardly
think of discussing it as part of the general stylistic procedure of its author: we should rather wish, beginning
with its language, to arrive at a comprehension of its
total form and meaning. And we should be much less
inclined to make a transition from the work to the mind
of the author for the simple reason that the work itself
is sufficiently complex and complete to command our
whole attention.

Period Style

The most obvious development of the individual style-

study is its extension to the style of a whole period.
This nevertheless presents certain difficulties. While we
are studying the work of one author we have a defined body of material to investigate; if we extend the
investigation to the work of a whole period we have
always far more material than can be dealt with. The
problem of selection immediately makes its appearance.
How is the selection to be made? If we choose to study
a period through the most strongly marked and
characteristic passages of its literature there is always a
danger of predetermining the state of the case. We choose
the evidence to suit an answer that we have already
in mind. This sometimes happens with the Romantic
poets. By focusing on illustrations drawn from, say, 'The
Ancient Mariner' and 'Resolution and Independence', we
tend to forget how much of the eighteenth century survives in Wordsworth and Coleridge, and how readily
they could slip back into the eighteenth-century manner
at times when their imaginative pressure was low. On
the other hand, we would all, I suppose, agree that the
style of a period is constituted by its most original
literary minds in their most vigorous moments—the
'Epistle to Arbuthnot', the close of the *Dunciad*, rather
than the undistinguished mass of couplet-writing at that
time; Dickens rather than Wilkie Collins.

Vocabulary, image, sentence-structure, the proportion
of nouns to adjectives, of nominal phrases to verbs—all
these things go to make up the characteristic flavour of a
period style; and they can all be investigated on a quantitative and statistical basis. If this is done the result may have
some claim to be scientific, but it is unlikely to be of much
literary significance. These difficulties came in the
works of Josephine Miles on period styles in English
poetry, to which we shall return. That we all have a
vague composite idea of the style of Augustan prose,

of the Romantic poetic vocabulary, is undoubtedly true; how far we can do anything to make this more precise, and how far it is worth doing, is another question. In individual style-studies we come to understand a work of art, or an individual artist's whole creative impulse; in period studies we can only arrive at that ill-defined and often self-contradictory abstraction, the mind of an age.

It is very noticeable that Continental students are far more inclined to hypostatize that abstraction, the style of a period, than we are in the English-speaking world. Serious attempts are made to define the Baroque, the Mannerist and the Rococo styles. It is noticeable that the terminology is borrowed from the visual arts: and many such studies seem to be an attempt to apply the methods that Wölfflin used in his *Principles of Art History* (1915) to the study of literature. In this book, of fundamental importance in its own field, Wölfflin distinguishes between the linear and the painterly, between plane and recession, between closed and open form, and so forth; and on this basis attempts the distinction between the styles of different periods. I cannot think of any good reason why the same methods should not be applied to literature, yet in practice the results of any such attempt always seem to be both arid and uncertain. It may be that in art history the illustrations can be more immediately and rapidly apprehended; it may be that in considering literature the isolation of particular qualities in this way forbids all proper consideration of meaning, and that style-study that fails to go on to the consideration of meaning is doomed to sterility. Perhaps there is a concreteness and particularity in the English literary mind that makes it radically unsympathetic to such studies. Certainly the best English work of this kind seems to occur in passing and in the course of doing other things; it also seems to move as rapidly as possible from the general to the particular. Geoffrey Tillotson gives us not generalizations about Augustan poetic diction, but a close and precise description of the language of Pope's descriptive and pastoral poetry; Helen Gardner abandons generalizations about Metaphysical poetry, and tends instead to show us the individuality and variety among the poets of that school.

In our literary climate definition, classification and labelling is apt to be thought of as a particularly barren exercise. To establish a concept of the Baroque or of Mannerism in literature, and then to assign Milton to the first and Donne to the second, seems neither convincing nor satisfying. But we may be wrong. I am often haunted by the suspicion that the art historians, with their schools and styles and periods, have a command of their material and of its development that literary historians seem to lack. And to many Continental students our unwillingness to deal in such ideas would seem but another example of our well-known incapacity for going beyond the barest empiricism.

All that has been said about the attempt to find the style of a period can be said with even more force about the attempt to define the style of a whole national literature. There was a time when it was seen as a virtue in an English writer to be characteristically English, but this belongs to a simple and comfortable patriotism rather than to literary intelligence. It has on the whole been left to the Germans to bring the study of specifically national styles into the range of serious intellectual endeavour. Examples of this occur in the work of Vossler, Curtius, and even occasionally in that of Spitzer. We tend to regard these endeavours with suspicion or indifference. Yet it cannot be doubted that there are national styles, and they may be legitimate objects of curiosity. There is a Frenchness about French literature;

we do feel in reading French poetry the presence of a complex of characteristics quite different from those that we experience in reading English poetry, and we are quite willing to talk about it, on a loose and conversational level. Yet both the desire and the equipment to bring this into the area of serious discussion are lacking. So far as these exercises are mere outbreaks of literary nationalism we may willingly dispense with them; yet we can imagine a serious study of the separate contributions of individual national literatures, seen as constituent parts of that great organism which Goethe conceived of as 'world literature'; and we can imagine that this might not be without its value. It does not, however, seem to be within the range of present possibilities.

History of Style

If it is difficult to arrive at a characterization of the style of a particular period, to write any consistent history of style seems more difficult still. We can trace the history of a single stylistic device, see how it changes in form and develops in function. We can, admitting the difficulties already mentioned, arrive at some sort of picture of the prevailing style of a particular epoch. But to move through the centuries on a broad and comprehensive front is virtually impossible; and all such attempts tend either to split up into unrelated fragments or to spread out into a swamp of generalization. To use Saussure's terminology, we have not yet found a way of combining the synchronic with the diachronic point of view, and perhaps we never shall. The best that can be done is take a series of cross-sections, or a series of typical examples, and place them side by side. This is not history, but it is perhaps the nearest we can get to it. There have been some notable examples of this, the pre-eminent one being Auerbach's *Mimesis*.

Apart from the difficulty of marshalling a mass of material relating to one period and keeping it all moving together through successive developments, there is the still greater difficulty of anomalous and irregular survivals. The style of imaginative prose in the early nineteenth century goes through many and rapid changes: but the style of expository writing hardly alters in any distinct way from that of the later eighteenth century, until the threshold of the modern period is reached. As we have remarked, there are similar survivals in poetry. The most popular and influential criticism is often misleading. The propaganda for a new classicism in the early part of this century would lead us to suppose that there was a complete break with Victorian stylistic tradition about 1914. And this has tended to obscure the presence of decidedly Tennysonian elements in the verse of T. S. Eliot, and the strong continuity between the verse of Browning and that of Pound. We have been led to suppose that Gerard Manley Hopkins was one of the founding fathers of the modern movement in poetry: yet actual traces of his stylistic influence are few. It looks very much as though such matters can be properly discussed only by tracing the development of individual poets.

Statistical Methods

Something should be said at this point about statistical methods of investigation, now becoming much more prominent with the use of computers. They are probably repugnant to most students of literature, Luddites by nature, as Lord Snow has observed. It is felt on the one hand that insensitive and inappropriate methods are introduced into literary scholarship by such means; on the other, that

literary students are unwilling to submit their observations to positive verification. Demarcation disputes are
not usually very rational affairs, but there are some real
questions to be asked and some answers can be given.
If it is asked whether statistical information is ever relevant to style-study the answer must be a qualified 'Yes'.
Nearly all criticism, even that most stigmatized as impressionistic, employs it in a loose and informal way.
If a critic remarks on Johnson's antithetical style, he
means in the end that more antitheses will be found in a
typical passage of Johnson than in a typical passage of,
say, Addison of similar length. This is finally a statistical
matter. By choosing a number of suitable passages and
doing the necessary calculation, the results could be expressed numerically as a statistical average—Johnson so
many antitheses per 2,000 words, Addison so many. And
this is only to put the original observation into numerical
form.

Has anything been gained by performing this opera-
tion? Here the answer is less simple. If there is any doubt
whether Johnson's style is actually marked by a free use
of antithesis, this is obviously the way to settle it. A
statement about the frequency of a particular stylistic
device will then have been verified by appropriate statistical methods; and these are the only methods by which it
could have been verified. Sometimes this is a real gain.
Received ideas about the style of a particular period or a
particular author sometimes turn out to have no basis in
fact when subjected to this kind of investigation. If snarks
can be shown to be boojums only by statistical analysis,
why then we must use it. In the Johnson case, which I
take to be an ordinary and typical one, I cannot see that
we are likely to gain anything. No one is in serious doubt
that Johnson did make frequent use of antithesis; and
for most literary purposes the common observation can

stand without further precision, just as the observation
that it is a cold day can stand without consulting the
thermometer. And the questions of literary importance
are likely to be how he used antithesis, what he did with
it, what part it plays in the total economy of his work—
none of these open to statistical investigation.

There are people who talk as though any gain in
numerical precision is valuable in itself. From the literary
point of view this is nonsense. Suppose (to keep to our
painfully over-simplified example) someone worked the
matter out and decided that the proportion of antitheses
in Johnson to those in Addison was 2 : 1. From a literary
point of view we should say. 'Yes Johnson uses far more',
as we had always seen'. Suppose now that a more pain-
staking investigator did the job again and discovered that
the count has been wrong, and that the proportion was
really 3 : 1 or 3 : 2. What difference would it make? None
at all. We should still say, 'Yes, Johnson uses far more,
as we had always known.' Nothing that the literary
judgment can make use of is contributed by these figures.

Some sort of statement about frequency of occurrence
is nevertheless necessary. If the use of a particular stylistic feature in a novel is being discussed, it makes a
difference whether it appears on every page, about once
in a chapter, or five times in the whole book. But it is
usually enough, as Stephen Ullmann has remarked in an
admirable passage on this matter, to note the significant
recurrence of some linguistic feature without inquiring
into precise numerical details. Insignificant figures, even
though they may in themselves do no particular harm,
tend to vitiate the quality of a whole argument by
implying claims to precision, or to a kind of precision,
that literary inquiry simply does not admit of.

The principal use of numerical criteria, as Ullman goes
on to point out, is in cases where style is examined not

E

for its own sake, but for some ulterior purpose—to settle questions of authorship, or to establish the chronology of an author's work. Statistical examination of sentence-lengths, frequency of certain words in the vocabulary, etc., can by comparison with an author's known work go far to determine the authenticity of doubtful works. These methods always fall short of complete certainty, but they can pile up an impressive body of inductive evidence. Such investigations deal only with positively identifiable characteristics, and commonly with characteristics which would not be apparent to ordinary direct observation; they deal with large numbers and large bodies of material; and there is no substitute for accurate statistical procedure. Formerly very laborious, many of these tasks—the making of concordances, word indexes, etc.—can now be done by computers; and it would be the merest superstition not to use them. Though it is notable that one of the best of these studies is also the earliest, well before the computer period: G. Udney Yule's statistical studies in the authorship of *The Imitation of Christ*. But the data provided by computers have only a small and peripheral place in literary study; and it is important that these machine-minding activities should be kept peripheral and small. Since they use elaborate apparatus, cost a great deal of money and can be pursued by persons of no literary culture whatever, they naturally acquire great prestige in forward-looking universities.

Older statistical methods were frequently uncertain of what they were counting and therefore liable to count wrong. From the latter part of the nineteenth century metrical tests of a statistical kind were employed in attempting to date Shakespeare's plays. The proportion of rhyme, of light endings and weak endings, were counted and used as criteria of date, as in a general way they quite properly can. But the precise nature of the data to be examined was often ill defined, and the statistical methods were extremely rough and ready. Even in such small and positive matters as these, no two observers seem to come up with the same results. No doubt we have reformed this indifferently with us: but there are some daunting examples of misplaced statistical fetishism even in quite recent years. Josephine Miles in her book *Eras and Modes in English Poetry* sets out to distinguish period styles by the proportion of verbal to substantival elements—roughly the proportion of verbs to nouns and adjectives. Those styles with a high proportion of verbs are called 'clausal', those with a high proportion of nouns and adjectives are called 'phrasal', and those in between are called 'balanced'. On this basis an elaborate historical scheme is evolved, with all the centuries behaving in a miraculously symmetrical manner. At the back of the book is a table of the English poets showing the proportion of adjectives, nouns and verbs in their work. This is set out in such a way that no easy comparison can be made between them—Dryden, 10; 19; 10; Prior, 12; 15; 9; Rossetti, 12; 15; 8. (It is not clear whether adjectives have any separate significance from nouns, but it is the proportion of verbs to nouns and adjectives taken together than is taken account of in the argument.) When by some tedious arithmetic we reduce the figures to a common denominator we find that the allegedly balanced Dryden has almost precisely the same proportion of verbs to nouns and adjectives as the allegedly phrasal Prior; and that the clausal Rossetti, who ought to have more verbs, has actually a higher proportion of nouns and adjectives. Keats and Shelley in a supposedly clausal period have a high proportion of nouns and adjectives. And so on. The figures are almost unreadable as they stand, and if reduced to an intelligible form make nonsense of the general argument.

The book as a whole is very far from nonsense: there is a real difference between dominantly verbal and dominantly nominal styles, and many interesting and important observations flow from this distinction. It reveals more about kinds than about periods—Pope and Thompson, coincident in time, show strikingly different proportions; but then they were writing different kinds of poetry: and the bare figures tell us almost nothing. Dryden's formula, 10; 19; 10, is exactly the same as that of Gerard Manley Hopkins: they are both balanced. Are we any the wiser for this? Does it show that they had anything important in common? Not at all. Everything that is valuable in the book comes in the qualitative discussions, which are frequently acute and perceptive. The method as a whole is a classic case of misplaced quantification.

The first question for literary students who feel tempted to embark on statistical methods is whether the numerical data that are looked for can contribute anything to the qualitative interpretation of style. If the answer is 'Yes', three simple rules might be added: (i) make a clear identification of what it is that is being counted; (ii) get the help of someone who can count right, or use a machine; (iii) make sure that the argument is actually supported by the figures. The application of these principles would banish most (not all) statistical arguments from literary studies to some other field, where we need not follow them.

4

Some practitioners

Leo Spitzer

In this chapter I shall consider some eminent modern
exponents of style-study in order to see how the general
principles already discussed work out in practice. The
choice of examples is necessarily selective, and with more
space many more might have been included. But I hope to
illustrate the principal trends which ought to be of interest to the English reader.

I shall begin by discussing the work of Leo Spitzer,
because he has a particularly well-developed method of
style-study and has expounded it in considerable detail.
Spitzer was one of the most distinguished of the German
literary scholars who were expelled by the Nazis, and
after the war found a new home in the United States. His
earlier work on Romance philology was entirely in the
German tradition; after he settled in America some concessions, though not many, were made to an Anglo-
Saxon audience. He was a man of immensely wide learning, not without pedantry; polemical and contentious
in his manner of writing, but with a passion for literature
and a profound and generous understanding of the roots
of Western culture. Himself a Jew and a Viennese, his
chosen field was the literature of the Romance languages,

and his intellectual allegiance was to a Hellenic-Christian tradition that he saw as a single entity. I have chosen a passage from his confession of faith as the epigraph to this book, both for its intrinsic appropriateness and as a tribute to his memory. He started, as we have seen, from a dissatisfaction on the one hand with the old comparative philology, on the other hand with purely external and positivist literary history. The first he found to have no connection with literature at all, while the second accumulated facts about literature—dates, attributions, influences and so forth—without ever penetrating to the heart of literature itself. These disillusionments might almost have led to the abandonment of literary study altogether; but they did not. They led instead to a growing conviction of the essential unity of literary and linguistic study; a belief that the study of language should lead to an understanding of the greatest achievements of language—works of literary art; and that works of literary art can only be understood by a minute study of the language in which they are realized. This is the theme of his book *Linguistics and Literary History*, for the English reader the best introduction to his work.

Spitzer remains always a philologist, in the extended German sense of the word; that is to say, a literary scholar, with equal emphasis on both members of the phrase—literature and scholarship. He had an equal contempt for dilettante or impressionist literary study and for the kind of scholarship that accumulates facts without adding anything to literary understanding. Although his work was extremely wide-ranging and his conclusions often more speculative and transcendental than is congenial to the English mind, he insisted strongly on the relative autonomy of literary studies. He disliked the tendency to disregard the philological character of the discipline of literary history, which is concerned with ideas couched in linguistic and literary form, not with ideas in themselves (this is the field of the history of philosophy). He distrusted the self-assurance with which students of literature undertake to treat complex subjects of a philosophic, political or economic nature and so turn their proper field into 'the gay sporting-ground of incompetence'. 'Only in the linguistic literary field,' he added, 'are we philologians competent *qua* scholars.' He even remained, to a large extent, a philologist in the narrower sense: much of his work was on historical semantics, and he was always anxious to start his literary inquiries from linguistic and etymological observations, even if their literary relevance seems on the face of it very slight.

The essential of his method is what he calls the philological circle—a method for which he adduces an elaborate genealogy in German hermeneutics that need not concern us here. The procedure is to argue from an observed detail to the central core of a work of art, and then to proceed outward from the centre in search of further confirmatory detail. The process can then be repeated as often as necessary until the limits of understanding have been reached. Two features in this method are especially to be observed. In the first place, it is opposed to the mere linear accumulation of observations, in the vague hope that some pattern will finally emerge from them. Secondly, the process is intuitive at two points. The initial observation is a spontaneous intuitive insight; it cannot be manufactured or enforced by a system. Some authentic connection between the observer and the work of art must establish itself spontaneously. If a particular student finds that this connection is absent, no amount of system or training will help him; he had better give up literature and do something else. And again, the passage from the observed peripheral fact to the central core is at first an intuitive leap, a hypothesis. A peculiar grammatical detail suggests a certain central orientation of the author's mind; and this is an informed surmise rather than a demonstration. We are rescued, however, from mere impressionism and subjectivity by returning outward from this central point and finding other details which will confirm and, if possible, refine the original hypothesis. In this way, a body of evidence is built up which will provide a view of the author's central creative attitude, or as the informing principle of a single work.

This is a good deal easier to explain than it is to illustrate in practice, for it is a description of a general approach rather than a rigid series of operations, and in an actual literary inquiry the paradigm is not often exhibited completely. Spitzer gives a simple illustration in the work of an elementary student of Latin construing a Ciceronian period: he can only do it by moving from a detail (the form of a particular word) to an assumed whole (the structure of the whole sentence) and then back to further details in order to confirm and build up the picture of the whole. I have little doubt that this represents truly both the aim and the method of literary inquiry. The aim is understanding, not new information: and the method is a continual to-and-fro movement between observable details and the hidden centre which we wish to reach, possess and comprehend. The end is an act of contemplation rather than the safe delivery of a package of facts.

It is not necessary that the starting-point should be a linguistic observation: it may be an observation about imagery or plot. Spitzer says somewhere that it was his own philological training that led him to adhere to the linguistic approach. As a matter of fact, he does not always adhere to it; but it remains his favoured method and he does seem to feel that the linguistic detail is the irreducible demonstrable fact which affords the securest anchorage for later speculations. And this conforms also to his conviction of the essentially philological character of literary study—that it cannot properly be short-circuited into history of ideas, psychology or a loose kind of philosophizing. As for value judgments, comparative or absolute, he is chary of them. For him, the primary task of the student is the *critique des beautés*, involving the prior acceptance of the work of art as a value in itself, to be apprehended in its totality:

Indeed, any *explication de texte*, any philological study, must start with a *critique des beautés*, with the assumption on our part of the perfection of the work to be studied and with an entire willingness to sympathy; it must be an apologia, a theodicy in a nutshell. . . . A criticism which insists on faults is justifiable only after the purpose of the author has been thoroughly understood and followed up in detail. The glibness with which critics, especially great German critics (Lessing, Schiller and Schlegel), have slandered French classical drama is only to be explained on the basis of premature judgments drawn from a quite extraneous comparison with Shakespeare. (*Linguistics and Literary History*, 128).

It is relevant to ask what kind of understanding Spitzer's work seeks to arrive at. In his earlier writing he tended to look for the meaning of the work of art in the mind of its author; his interpretation was largely a psychological one. It was the guiding spirit, the central spring of the author's imagination, that the observation of linguistic details was supposed to lead to; and there was a distinct and acknowledged Freudian influence on his investigations. Later, perhaps under the influence (never acknowledged) of a more modern and more sophisticated Anglo-American criticism, he came to distinguish

more clearly between the creative imagination and the
historic personality of the author, and between the work
of art and the mind of its creator. His object then became
rather to explain the inner being of the work itself; but
for him this always remained quite clearly what the
author meant to put into it. He was severe about the
incorporation into hermeneutics of later accretions of
meaning and was quite willing to talk in terms of the
author's purpose. I never heard him speak of those opponents of the 'intentional fallacy' whose views were
much in the air in his later days: but the whole tenor,
expressed and unexpressed, of his work was to think of
the author's intention as something specific, definite and,
in principle, discoverable. To discover it was indeed the
business of stylistics.

Spitzer's method has been the object of a great deal
of criticism, and his philological circle was frequently
denounced as a vicious one. The general tendency can
be indicated by a quotation from Professor Harold
Cherniss—though this passage was actually directed at
scholars of the Stefan George school rather than at
Spitzer himself:

The intuition which discovers in the writings of an author
the natural law and inward form of his personality, is proof
against all objections, logical and philological; but while
one must admit that a certain native insight, call it direct
intelligence or intuition, as you please, is required for
understanding any text, it is all the same a vicious circle
to intuit the nature of the author's personality from his
writings, and then to interpret those writings in accord-
ance with the inner necessity of that intuited personality
(ibid., 34).

Spitzer's reply was to disembarrass the idea of intuition
from any transcendental or mystical overtones: intuition, as he understands it, is simply a gifted and informed

perception. He then goes on to remark that though the method is indeed circular the circle is not vicious, but benign. The intuitive leap from the surface detail to the assumed centre is checked by a return to the surface and the observation of further details; and so on until the whole has been grasped. It is this repeated series of movements that rescue the process from mere subjective and unverifiable private judgment.

A more serious criticism to my mind is that the link between the linguistic starting-point and the literary insight is often a tenuous one. In some of his writing the preliminary linguistic work looks too much like a series of conjurer's passes, designed to mislead the spectator about what is actually going on. After we have been suitably dazzled by a display of linguistic sleight of hand, a black cloth is held up in front of the top-hat, and when it is withdrawn an admirable but wholly irrelevant rabbit is pulled out. And this, I think, points to one of the cardinal difficulties of stylistics. Stylistics claims— must claim—that the understanding of a work of literary art is continuous with the understanding of its language, and that the close, even technical, study of language is the only sure way to literary understanding. Many critics, while paying lip-service to this view, actually tend to take short-cuts, and proceed to interpret works of literature in moral or ideological terms, without considering linguistic texture in any detail at all. And it sometimes seems that Spitzer's conclusions are those of the scholarly man of letters, that they depend more on wide literary experience, a large range of comparisons, deep knowledge of cultural history, rather than on any expertise that could be called philological in the narrower sense. It is a not uncommon dilemma; stylistics stays firmly within its own terms of reference, and is condemned to triviality: or it proceeds to ideas of great scope and generality by deserting strictly stylistic methods.

But much of Spitzer's work bears witness that this need not be so. The brilliant study of the style of Diderot, for example, begins from some observations on rhythm—a breathless, accelerating, almost feverish rhythm to be found in a passage of Diderot's writing, almost as though it were patterned on the rhythm of the sexual act. This observation is fused with a consideration of the subject-matter of the passage; other passages of a different tenor are brought into the argument until a vision of Diderot's imaginative activity as a whole is reached, quite transcending common critical objections to its fragmentary and incoherent quality. In the study of *Don Quixote* the starting-point is the variability and uncertainty about the naming of the characters. The various names for a single character are then seen as reflections of various points of view from which he can be regarded. From this we pass by links which I confess are sometimes not easy to follow, to the prevalence of varied, shifting and uncertain viewpoints in the whole work: so that in the end the essence of the book is seen to be characterized by this perspectivism.

It is sometimes the case that the stylistic observations lead to a conclusion not very different from that reached impressionalistically by common literary opinion. Spitzer is prepared for this:

Sometimes it may happen that this etymology leads simply to a characterization of the author that has long been accepted by literary historians (who have not needed apparently to follow the winding path I chose), and which can be summed up in a phrase which smacks of a college handbook. But to make our way to an old truth is not only to enrich our own understanding : it produces inevitably new evidence of objective value for this truth—which is thereby renewed (ibid., 38).

Sometimes the initial observation is not of a peculiarly linguistic kind. The magnificent interpretation of a passage from Claudel's *Cinq Grandes Odes* begins by analysing the structure of what at first seems a rhapsodic poem, singularly resistant to analysis. It is true that Spitzer finds the clue to the structure in the punctuation provided by the word *grand* six times repeated at critical points. But this verbal clue is of the slightest: and what we arrive at in the end is a superb and deeply felt interpretation of the five odes as a whole, seen as a single great poem. But here the difficulty was to find a way into this daunting and almost impenetrable piece. Spitzer's claim is that the slightest linguistic observation may serve as a point of entry. It does not matter what it is as long as the observation is genuine and original. No system or predetermined scheme can serve as a guide. It is here, I believe, that the freshness and liberating power of Spitzer's recommendation is to be found. The student or aspiring interpreter is free to make his way into the work by any route that native wit or temperamental inclination may offer. His duty is then to pursue his course with rigour, pertinacity and complete submission, not to any predetermined code of rules, but to the work of art as it presents itself, secure in the belief that the work is an organic whole and that the extended study of any part of it must lead to an understanding of the whole.

It is my firm belief, corroborated by the experience of many exercises practised in seminars with my students, when I chose to start from any particular point suggested by one of the group, that any one good observation will, when sufficiently deepened, infallibly lead to the centre of the work of art. There are no preferential vantage-points (such as the ideas, the structure of the poem, etc.) with which we are obliged to start: any well-observed item can become a vantage-point and however arbitrarily chosen must, if rightly developed, ultimately lose its arbitrariness (ibid., 198).

And the end of the whole process? Here Spitzer's claims are essentially modest. He is not out to build a critical system or expound a philosophy, but simply to understand the work on its own terms—an understanding that could ideally be arrived at without any exegesis at all. He concludes the Claudel study by saying:

Stylistics as I conceive it is an exclusively auxiliary science. Just as, according to Pascal, for him who knows truth no style, no *art de persuader* is needed, so stylistics must abdicate once the true nature of the work of art has been perceived. A study of the kind we have attempted could have been made entirely unnecessary from the start by a simple recital of the poem, if the performer were able, by various pauses and intonations, to suggest the main motifs we have taken pains to distinguish, and to show within the crystalline ball of the work of art the play of the conflicting forces in the equilibrium which Claudel has been able to establish.

Erich Auerbach

Next to Spitzer it is appropriate to consider the work of Erich Auerbach. His formation and personal history were closely similar to Spitzer's. After already distinguished careers in Germany, both worked in Turkish universities during the Nazi period, and after the war both settled in the United States. In Auerbach's case it is largely this period of relative isolation in Turkey that brings him within the scope of our study. Also a Romance philologist by vocation, his orientation was on the whole more historical than Spitzer's, and he was less exclusively devoted to *explication de texte*. His magisterial essay 'Figura', for example, begins as a semantic investigation into the significance of the word, and develops into a profound study of Christian typology, its motives and its procedures. But it is not tied to any particular literary text. Working in Istanbul with limited library facilities, he was increasingly forced back to concentrate on the texts themselves; and with this stimulus he began to put together, under the domination of a single idea, a number of studies of individual texts, of widely differing periods, varying from Homer and the Old Testament to the Goncourts and Virginia Woolf. The result of this is his great book *Mimesis*, probably the most profound, most learned, and most wide-ranging work of style-study that has ever been written. The dominant idea is given in the sub-title of the book, 'The Representation of Reality in Western Literature'. Its scope is enormous—nothing less than the various ways in which men's actual experience, historical, social, moral and religious, has been represented in literary form in all the various phases of Western culture. It was only the limits imposed by his situation that made this study possible. As he says himself, 'it is quite possible that the book owes its existence to just this lack of a rich and specialized library. If it had been possible for me to acquaint myself with all the work that has been done on so many subjects, I might never have reached the point of writing.'

As it is, the range of learning is formidable; and it is hard to believe that the educational situation of post-war Europe will ever produce anything like it again. But it is all concentrated on the study of particular passages, all of them comparatively short. Auerbach has this to say about his procedure:

The method of textual interpretation gives the interpreter

a certain leeway. He can choose and emphasize as he pleases. It must naturally be possible to find what he claims in the text. My interpretations are no doubt guided by a specific purpose. Yet this purpose assumed form only as I went along, playing, as it were, with my texts, and for long stretches of my way I have been guided only by the texts themselves. Furthermore, the great majority of the texts were chosen at random, on the basis of accidental acquaintance and personal preference, rather than in view of a definite purpose. Studies of this kind do not deal with laws, but with trends and tendencies, which cross and complement each other in the most varied ways. I was by no means interested merely in presenting what would serve my purpose in the narrowest sense; on the contrary, it was my endeavour to accommodate multiplex data and to make my formulations correspondingly elastic (*Mimesis*, 491).

The result is probably unique in its combination of the synchronic with the diachronic approach, in doing full justice to the individual being of individual works, yet at the same time giving a valid and substantiated picture of historical development. The only pity is that so few scholars are likely to have the equipment to emulate it. Most style-studies have been, perhaps naturally, studies of individual works, individual authors or limited tendencies. Spitzer, for example, seems to have flitted from flower to flower in the immense meadow of Romance literature without thinking of tracing a connected route; and his books are simply assemblages of separate and separately published papers. Each of the studies that go to form *Mimesis* has the density and particularity of an individual learned article, but the whole is directed by a single purpose, and from the great mass of varied critical scholarship an unforced but coherent pattern can be seen to emerge. Furthermore, the connection between the linguistic observations—remarks on vocabulary or syntax—and the wider considerations to which they lead is always clear. Auerbach is ultimately a historian of culture, and he arrives in the end at conclusions of great scope and generality. But he always founds these wider considerations securely on a linguistic base. If, as I have suggested, the methods of stylistics are sometimes open to question, we have at least in *Mimesis* a triumphant vindication of their proper use.

It would be impossible to summarize the content of this book, as it contains twenty separate essays, on topics ranging over a span of 3,000 years. All that can be done here is to indicate the procedure in one or two of the separate studies, and the main general argument that emerges from the whole. The first essay contrasts a passage of Homer—the recognition of Odysseus by Euryclea, the old nurse—with a story from the Old Testament, the sacrifice of Isaac. In the Homeric narrative everything is in the foreground, uniformly illuminated; the place, the setting, the identity of the characters clearly indicated. When a passage of reminiscence is introduced, as it is in the lines describing how Odysseus came by his scar, this in its turn becomes foreground, equally clear, present and objective. With this Auerbach contrasts the biblical narrative, beginning with a dialogue between Abraham and God. It is located nowhere; God has no physical being. We know nothing of his purpose; He has not, like Zeus, discussed it in Council with the other gods. Yet a sense of purpose and significance, that yet remains obscure and mysterious, enfolds the whole narrative. This is only the starting-point of a full and elaborate differentiation; but it is also the starting-point for a contrast that runs through the whole book:

The two styles, in their opposition, represent basic types: on the one hand fully externalized description, uniform

F

illumination, uninterrupted connection, free expression, all events in the foreground, displaying unmistakable meaning, few elements of historical development and of psychological perspective; on the other hand, certain parts brought into high relief, others left obscure, abruptness, suggestive influence of the unexpressed, background quality, multiplicity of meaning and the need for interpretation, universal historical claims, development of the concepts of the historically becoming, and preoccupation with the problematic (ibid., 19).

In succeeding essays, later styles are discussed— Petronius, Tacitus, Ammianus Marcellinus—to illustrate how a formal and elaborate rhetoric is employed on increasingly irrational, crude and violent material, leading up to the crisis of style in which this tension finally culminated. One of the central points of the book is the strict separation of styles in classical literature: the high style for noble subjects, the low style for comic and vulgar material. Where is it that common men, speaking in common language, without the graces of rhetoric, are nevertheless represented as engaging in affairs of the greatest weight, seriousness and moment? Not anywhere in classical literature: it is in the Bible, especially in the Gospels, that we find this mixing of styles, always heterodox from the classical point of view. The reverberations of this contrast are clearly felt throughout the whole of Western literature and Western culture; and this must serve as a brief illustration of the way in which a stylistic observation can lead to cultural and historical considerations of a fundamental kind.

The classical, patristic and medieval periods, and the intellectual links which bind them together, are probably Auerbach's preferred field; but he passes on, via studies of Rabelais, Montaigne, Cervantes, Saint-Simon and many others, to consider modern realism. This he finds to be a distinct new development, different from the Christian realism of the Bible and the Middle Ages. It is the self-consciousness and rapid acceleration of social change inaugurated by the French Revolution that gives rise to modern realism; and Auerbach traces its varieties in Stendhal, Balzac, Flaubert and the Goncourts. He concludes with a brief glance at the disintegration of traditional methods of representation in modern literature, illustrated from a passage of Virginia Woolf; but it is only a brief glance; and he does not disguise his conviction that the history of Western culture, as he and his generation have understood it, is fast drawing to an end.

He may be right. However that may be, it is notable that neither he nor Spitzer has had much dealing with distinctively modern literature, nor with literature in English. Spitzer can be positively wrong in interpreting even traditional English literature, as he is in his reading of Donne's 'Ecstasy'; or naïvely eager to make a gesture of accommodation to a new world, as in his essay on 'American Advertising as Popular Art'. Auerbach, so vigorously at home in earlier centuries, seems to work under a slowly darkening elegiac cloud as he approaches modern times. It is possible, therefore, to admire the methods of these two writers, to be awed by their scholarship, and still to feel that there is plenty left to do on similar lines by those who could not hope to compete with them on their own ground.

Damaso Alonso

The work of Damaso Alonso is of a rather different character from that of Spitzer and Auerbach, for it has been confined to Spanish poetry, particularly the poetry of the *Siglo d'Oro*. Of this my ignorance is almost complete, so what I have to say about his writing must be partial and external. But his book, *Poesia Español*, has its sub-title, 'Ensayo de Metodos y Limitos Estilisticos', and the theoretical considerations interspersed among the particular studies are of great general interest. I should like to believe that they have not been without effect on my own thinking, such as it is, since I first made their acquaintance nearly twenty years ago; and they should certainly be better known to English readers. Many links will be observed with the methods of Saussure and Bally, against which Alonso's work is a reaction; and with the methods of Spitzer, to which it shows some similarities.

Alonso begins by accepting a classification from Saussure's terminology, but rejecting its clear-cut oppositions. Saussure calls the complete linguistic phenomenon a 'sign': and the sign unites two elements, the signified and the signifier, which he defines as a concept and an acoustic image respectively. Alonso says that an *insalvable abismo* separates him from this way of looking at the matter. For Saussure the signified is a concept; the signifiers are simply conveyers or transmitters of concepts. This, Alonso says, is an idea 'as aseptic as it is poverty-stricken', far from the three-dimensional reality of language. In fact, the signifiers do not transmit concepts, but delicate functional complexes, including associations, synaesthesias, affective charges. We cannot consider the signified as merely conceptual. Indeed, we cannot isolate it. When a mother calls 'Jackie!' to her child she may do so affectionately, or angrily, or apprehensively because he is about to run under a lorry. In these cases what is the essential signified—the tone, the intensity, the speed, or what? In a line of verse the stress may be a signifier, the value of a single vowel sound may be one. The whole line with its rhythm, its accents, its vowel pattern and its conceptual contents is a complex signifier which arouses in us a complex signified. The signified is not essentially a concept; it is an intuition which produces an immediate modification of some elements, possibly every element, of our psyche. One of the elements will be conceptual, but others will not. Besides the departure from Saussure, it will be observed how clearly Alonso separates himself from Bally, with his basic distinction between the logical and affective aspects of language.

For stylistic purposes Alonso would substitute a distinction between outer form and inner form. Outer form is the relation of signifier to signified from the point of view of the signifier. The inner form is the same relation seen from the point of view of the signified. The study of outer form is the easier, for it starts from concrete phonetic realities. The study of the inner form is more difficult, for, as Alonso sees it, it deals with the psychology of the moment of creation, the moment of internal formation of the signified, and its immediate embodiment in a signifier. The stylistics of the future, he says, if there is to be any, will tend to an equal emphasis on both perspectives, outer and inner. It is easy to see that this has something in common with Spitzer's method of working from an exterior linguistic detail to the internal form of a whole work.

For Alonso there are three modes of understanding literary work, marked by an increasing degree of precision. The first is the understanding of the common reader, who seeks neither to analyse nor to exteriorize his impressions. It is a totalizing intuition, which forms itself in the process of reading and comes to reproduce the totalizing intuition which gave rise to the work—that is, the intuition of the author. Like Spitzer, Alonso is quite clear that the object of literary study is to recover the author's original purpose, though he perhaps expresses himself less in terms of conscious purpose. This 'reader's understanding' is immediate and intuitive, and it is the purer the fewer extraneous elements have come between reader and author. This means, I take it, that pure literary understanding is independent of external information—biographical, bibliographical, historical, etc. And this 'reader's understanding' is intransitive; it does not attempt to express itself. It is a simple relation between reader and work; its primary object is delight, and in delight it terminates. It is, of course, the indispensable foundation of all other kinds of literary understanding.

The second degree of understanding is that of the critic. There is a type of man in whom the qualities of the reader are exceptionally developed: his receptive capacity is both more intense and more extended than the ordinary. This exceptional creature is the critic. Ideally the range and intensity of his reactions should correspond with those of the poets themselves; and reading should incite in him profound and luminous intuitions, comprehending the work in its totality. Above all, the critic is a receptive apparatus of the greatest delicacy and amplitude.

But the critic has also, as a natural tendency of his personality, an expressive activity. He must communicate, compactly and rapidly, images of the intuitions he has received. This is his mission. He transmits his reactions, but they are not in themselves a problem for him. In general, it does not interest him to establish how or why these reactions have been produced. He is content with some general classificatory scheme that will enable him to communicate his intuitions to a reader of the same poem. Strictly speaking, these aesthetic intuitions are ineffable; all the same, the critic does his best to express them in a creative and poetic fashion. Criticism is an art.

It will be evident from this that Alonso severely limits the positive and scientific pretentions of criticism, and

is more than willing to find room for the impressionist
criticism that our century has often been inclined to
condemn. What he does not find room for, any more
than Spitzer does, is conventional literary history. There
are true literary works and false; the only true literary
works are those which have something to say and say it
directly to the heart of man. The true literary work is
ahistoric and cannot be the object of history, but there
is a monotonous mass of secondary works which say
nothing to the heart or mind of man; these form a vast
necropolis full of dead imitations. And this is the object
of what is commonly called literary history. But it is not
really literary history; it is the history of literary culture,
which is a different thing. Criticism is not concerned with
it. The discrimination of the true from the false literary
work has always been considered the principal function of
criticism.

In practice a distinction must be made between
criticism of the literature of the past and criticism of
contemporary literature. The criticism of past literature
is a continuous collective process. Sudden devaluations
and denigrations are an impossibility. Humanity will not
suddenly abandon the estimate of centuries for an upstart
fashion. The collective valuation has become itself an
intuition for humanity, and no individual judgment can
overturn it. The first function of criticism is not to re-
direct literary judgment, but to remove the rust of centuries, to explain changes of language, meaning, customs,
allusions, etc. And for this the intuitive insight of the
critic is not enough; he needs also a reasonable erudition.
The criticism of contemporaries is a different matter:
it is always and necessarily an unreliable affair, especially
criticism of the work of an immediately preceding generation. However, from an infinite rosary of judgments, all

inexact, that men make on their immediate circumstances, *Dios integra su verdad*, God composes his truth, the single criticism on which no one can cast doubt.

But there is a third stage in the understanding of literary works which goes beyond that of the critic. If we begin to ask, 'Why does this poem, or verse, move me? What is it, whence does it originate this emotion that passes through me, whence does it proceed?' we begin to pass to this third kind of understanding. Criticism answers these questions only in the vaguest and most general fashion because the problem does not really interest it: it is enough for the critic to make a rapid evaluative survey of his intuitions. His conclusions are intuitive and unscientific.

But we can at least begin to go farther, to our third stage, and consider the possibility of a scientific understanding of artistic facts. This scientific approach is stylistics. Typological classification solves nothing: it is the individual work that must be examined; and the final act of apprehension must always be an intuition. But stylistics offers the possibility of a precise and demonstrable analysis.

The poem presents itself to us on the one hand as a temporal succession of sounds—the signifiers; on the other as a spiritual content—the signified. The signified is a modification of our spiritual life, difficult to penetrate or to analyse. The total signifier A is linked to the total signified B by numerous partial links:

$$A \quad a_1 \; a_2 \; a_3 \; . \; . \; . \; a_n$$
$$| \quad | \quad | \quad | \qquad \quad |$$
$$B \quad b_1 \; b_2 \; b_3 \; . \; . \; . \; b_n$$

The first function of stylistics is to investigate the relation between the two wholes by investigating the relation between all the partial elements. The complete relation will be arrived at by integrating all these partial relations. These separate elements are very numerous—far too numerous for complete study. A selection must be made of those which are most relevant and most revealing. There is no cut-and-dried method available here; the selection can only be intuitive. This is evidently the same as Spitzer's principle of the personal intuitive observation as the point of entry into the work, and it shows the same objection to uniform and mechanical methods.

We begin stylistic investigation with the outer form—the signifier—because this is the concrete fact presented to our sense-perception. We consider the inner form—the signified—as a complex of elements: conceptual, affective, synaesthetic and image-producing; and we assert that the same complexity must exist in the signifier. The passage from the outer to the inner form is difficult, but it is precisely the object of stylistics to make it. Like Spitzer, Alonso sees the understanding to be attained partly in psychological terms. Indeed, he says that the literary investigator must double his role with that of the psychologist. He has to classify and study all the elements that have touched the spirit of the poet, all the elements which may have determined a certain reaction in him. We may add, parenthetically, that it is not easy to see how this can be done without passing outside the stylistic realm. However, Alonso insists that the aim of stylistics is to establish a rigorous and concrete link between signifier and signified, and so reach a full and accurate understanding of the total sign—that is to say, the total literary existence of the work. Stylistics so considered is the science of literature, and it is the only possible route to a true philosophy of literature. At present this science is limited and immature. All sorts of mixtures and combinations of criticism and stylistics are possible in practice and the one does not supersede the other. No one can be an investigator in stylistics who has not first been a passionate reader and secondly a devoted critic. We must always remember the three stages—the readers' knowledge which leads to an intuitive pleasure; the critics' knowledge, which has a pedagogical intention, and stylistic knowledge which leads to the solution of a problem. And for the final stage, the first two are always necessary.

1. A. Richards

When we pass from the work of the Continental European scholars to work in English, certain distinguishing features become very evident. The first, and to my mind the most important, is a sense of ecumenical range in this Continental scholarship, even when it is dealing with a particular national literature. Auerbach sees the whole of Western culture from the Old Testament to the threshold of modern times as a single object of contemplation; Spitzer says that philologists are in essence theologians, studying an eternal truth; Damaso Alonso says that out of a series of partial literary judgments, all inexact, *Dios integra su verdad*. We should perhaps not make too much of the theological reference in the last two utterances; what is striking is the sense of a whole culture with a single and indisputable authority, transcending temporary fashion and individual opinion. This seems to me a more informed and authentic commitment than the appeal to tradition common in the Anglo-American writing of the thirties, which was often used merely polemically in support of quite untraditional attitudes. And in the work of I. A. Richards and his successors the sense of long-established authority is wholly absent. The appeal is to a science that is supposed to be quite novel, to semantics or to a new experimental psychology, an enlightenment that dawned only yesterday, sometimes to mere bright ideas that serve an immediate purpose—to solve a local problem, to cast a new light on a particular text, to dazzle the sophomores, quite without integration into any comprehensive scheme of knowledge. I do not want to say this, and for myself I should wish to work for a state of affairs in which for England it would no longer be true, but as far as literary study is concerned the belief of General de Gaulle seems to be only too well founded—*les Anglo-Saxons* do seem to stand outside Europe.

In this matter of range and authority the advantage seems clearly to be with Europe. In another respect I am less certain. Spitzer and Alonso both see the ultimate goal of their research and the ultimate authority for their judgment in the intention of the author, which they regard as something final and, in principle, discoverable. Anglo-American work, whether criticism or stylistics in Damaso Alonso's sense, tends to be more sceptical about this possibility, and tends to allow far more for the accretion of meaning to a work of art with the passage of the centuries. It could justify this attitude by saying that any later accretion of meaning must in some sense have been latent in the original. The Anglo-American procedure would also make far more concessions to historical relativism. Whatever is true about a work of art is true only for the state of culture and society that sees it to be so. And this tendency has been accentuated by the Empsonian conception of ambiguity, of multiple meaning, even though the concept was not arrived at via historical considerations, but by a strictly stylistic, internal examination of the way that poetry works. The ideas of multiple meaning and accretion of meaning obviously give room for subjectivism, fantasy and eccentricity; but this may be a justifiable risk. Great liberty of interpretation

may in the end do more justice to the depth and multi-
fariousness of complex works of art.

Finally, the distinction between criticism and stylistics,
made explicitly by Damaso Alonso and at least implied
by Spitzer, is much less clear in English writing. The
critics have made considerable use of stylistic analysis;
and literary stylistics with a formal linguistic base is
hardly found among writing in English. With these pre-
liminaries, we can turn to the work of I. A. Richards.

A large part of Richards's writing does not concern us
here; his *Principles of Literary Criticism* and his writing
on literary theory in general are outside our field. The
important work is *Practical Criticism*, a book which has
the distinction of setting stylistics on a new footing almost without reference to hereditary literary disciplines.
Its results are not repugnant to the consensus of former
literary judgment; they would be self-condemned if they
were. But they have been arrived at by new methods and
were announced in a new tone. Indeed, the tone of
Practical Criticism often contrives to suggest that literary
interpretation had never seriously been undertaken before, or that all previous attempts at it were quite
negligible. This is not true; but it is true that Richards's
work is just about contemporary with new procedures
in stylistics in Europe, and so it is part of a general phase
of innovation. Richards's *Principles* first appeared in 1924,
Practical Criticism in 1927; Bally's *Traité de stylistique
française* first appeared in 1920, *Le langage et la vie*
in 1925; and in some respects, though by very different
methods, they were pursuing the same ends. Both assumed
that the logical and grammatical aspects of language had
received a good deal of study already and both wished
to turn their attention to the affective element of linguistic expression; but Bally approached this from orthodox
linguistics, Richards from semantics and psychology—as

such subjects were understood at that now rather distant period.

They were also addressing a different audience. Saussure, Bally and the Continental writers on stylistics generally were addressing their peers, scholars in language and literature. They did not feel it necessary to make concessions to ignorance or inexperience. Richards made his experiment in controlled reading with a class largely composed of undergraduates, and seems to be addressing his book to a general audience. He says he wrote *Practical Criticism* 'for those who were interested in the contemporary state of culture, whether as critics, as philosophers, as teachers, as psychologists or merely as curious persons'. The wide spread of his potential readers means that he cannot presume in them any real body of shared experience or any high degree of literary sophistication. This sometimes gives his writing an air of *naïveté*, of which it would not be hard to find examples. However, I do not think we should be too eager to search them out, for they are perhaps necessary consequences of another endeavour, immensely valuable in itself and quite unrepresented in Continental writing. That is the endeavour to find out from the beginning what the process of reading and interpreting poetry is really like; what actually goes on in the reader's mind; what are the obstacles to better understanding. This involves asking a number of awkward questions and exposing a number of unwelcome truths; and even if the later consequences have not been as uniformly salutary as might have been hoped, we have every reason to be grateful that the basic elementary difficulties of literary interpretation have been so fully exposed.

The procedure of *Practical Criticism* is by now familiar to everyone who is concerned with these matters. A number of short poems or extracts from longer poems were presented to the members of a large university class, without any indication of authorship or date, and they were asked to comment on them. The comments (which Richards, for some impenetrable reason, calls 'protocols') were collected, classified and analysed; and from this body of information an extended series of deductions was made about actual reading habits, about the methods and criteria that readers actually employed, and as a consequence about the state of literary education. As everyone knows, the results were disturbing. Incomprehension, capricious and eccentric judgment, and sheer, helpless bewilderment were found to be frequent. But I shall not enlarge on this, as it is a matter of general educational history rather than of stylistics. It must be realized from the start, however, that the conditions of the experiment were severely limited. Historical knowledge, the foundation of traditional opinion, the sense of an accepted literary tradition were as far as possible excluded by the dateless and anonymous character of the extracts presented. This was a necessary condition for the particular inquiry in hand: it was not a recommendation that such knowledge should be excluded for ever, or an assertion of its irrelevance. It is necessary to emphasize this, for the wide extension of 'practical criticism' methods as an educational procedure has led to the absurd idea that there is some special virtue in approaching literature divorced from its historical setting, that no knowledge of this is necessary, or, in more extreme cases, that there isn't really anything to know. Of course, Richards did not intend anything of this kind. Both Spitzer and Alonso at a later date have emphasized that the contact between the reader and the work must be effected by a kind of intuitive click; it is not a matter of imported external knowledge. Richards, much earlier, is setting himself to inquire how this intuitive click takes place. What are the connections that form themselves between the reader and the work, and what ought they to be?

Many of the obstacles to true interpretation disclosed by Richards' experiment were below the level of literary skill on which our Continental scholars were operating. Incomprehension of the plain sense, misjudgment of the feeling, half-baked and misinformed notions about metrics and poetical kinds, all discovered to be widespread, are part of educational pathology. What is of interest for stylistics is the ensuing analysis of literary meaning. Like Bally in *Le langage et la vie* and Damaso Alonso in *Poesia Española*, Richards insists that meaning cannot be reduced to conceptual meaning; the affective and expressive sides of language are also a part of meaning, and a part that has been damagingly neglected. No apparatus for examining it has ever been provided, and this Richards aims to supply.

He divides meaning into four aspects, which he calls sense, feeling, tone and intention. *Sense* is conceptual meaning: Bally's logical or intellectual aspect of language. 'We use words to direct our hearers' attention upon some state of affairs, to present to them some items for consideration, to excite in them some thought about these items.' The three other kinds of meaning represent a classification of Bally's affective and expressive aspects of language; and they are a clear improvement on Bally's very general terminology. *Feeling* is the emotional attitude towards the subject presented by sense. *Tone* directs our attention differently; it is the attitude not towards the subject, but towards the person addressed, actually or in imagination. *Intention* is the purpose, conscious or unconscious, of the whole utterance, the effect that the writer intended to promote. Sense and feeling probably need little further comment. Of tone we may say that it is obviously powerful. Richards remarks acutely that Gray's *Elegy* is largely a triumph of exquisitely adjusted tone. Intention presents a difficulty in that it can often be subsumed under one of the other three functions. The intention of a scientific paper is almost entirely a matter of sense; the intention of a love-letter is to convey feeling. But in many cases, particularly in literature, we need to consider intention as a distinct controlling factor. There is an obvious class of external intentions, such as that of the political speech that is made for the purpose of getting a certain party elected. Any interpretation of such a speech must take this controlling purpose into account. And in literature such extra-curricular intentions are not absent. But characteristically in literature we need to consider intention in another way: Is the passage under consideration addressed directly from author to reader, or is it a dramatic utterance spoken by a fictional character with whom the author does not identify himself? Or, to introduce examples that Richards does not, is it governed by certain over-riding conventions, such as the decorum of neo-classical tragedy, or the traditional praise of a lady in courtly love poetry? Obviously, both the choice and ordering of material is profoundly affected by such intentions as these, and obviously any stylistic analysis will go astray if they are not taken into account.

Literary meaning is characteristically a fusion of these four functions. By abstraction they can be considered separately, and in the process of stylistic inquiry they must be so considered. But the total meaning is the integration into a unity of all four. By this piece of analysis-and-synthesis, Richards has provided a simple and workable instrument of stylistic inquiry—so simple that it can be employed by students of literature at a very elementary stage, so fundamental that it cannot be neglected by even the most complex and sophisticated

literary interpretation. It can be objected that the analysis
does not go far enough. Richards shows a strong tendency
to set conceptual meaning on one side, and to bundle
all other sorts of meaning together as emotive. This is
more evident in the *Principles* than in *Practical Criticism*,
but it is a pervasive element in his thinking, and, looked
at more closely, the emotive label turns out not to be
satisfactory. It often calls a halt to further inquiry just
where inquiry is needed. Much of what Richards classi-
fies as feeling and tone can be analysed into different
aspects of sense. This objection has been taken up by
William Empson, and I think it is well founded; but for
all that, Richards's approach is clear, compact and usable.
It is, no doubt, a formalization of what the skilful interpreter has always done; but there is an immense gain
in having it set forth in this lucid and serviceable form.

Much of *Practical Criticism* is concerned with the
obstacles to just interpretation—doctrinal prejudice, the
domination of received ideas, partial and ill-informed
notions about literary form. These are of great interest
and undeniable educational importance, but rather aside
from our present theme. Much of its message is conveyed
in detailed discussion of the poems and in discussion of
the comments on them; and this it is impossible to summarize. It remains to say something about the limitations
of Richards's approach and the lines on which it has been
developed in the hands of others. Richards makes much
of the contribution of psychology to literary interpretation. But the psychology employed is not of a very ad-
vanced order, and I think it will seem to most readers
today that the real novelty of Richards's method is a
willingness to consider the internal processes of reading
and interpreting as they actually are, rather than any
importation of esoteric psychological knowledge. This
means a continual emphasis on what goes on in the

G

reader's mind; and at first sight it seems as though this takes us away from the poem towards the psychology of the audience. On this there are two things to be said. First, this orientation is a necessary consequence of Richards's particular purpose, which was not, as we have seen, a purely stylistic investigation. Secondly, and without going into any theoretical considerations about the mode of being of a work of literary art, the report of a reader's reaction to a poem, if sufficiently detailed, refined and controlled, is in practice tantamount to a description of the poem. And the effect of Richards's method, if rightly understood, is indeed to bring about, at least initially, that submission to the poem on its own terms that is recommended by a more traditional interpreter like Spitzer.

However, there is a difference. In Richards this submission is only initial, and his procedure is decidedly oriented towards judgment. His selection of pieces included bad and trivial poems as well as good ones, and he is much concerned with the means of discriminating between them. In general, stylistics has not thought much along these lines. It has been content to accept the historical literary canon, and to examine only works that it assumed to have excellence in their own kind. Spitzer, for example, is on principle extremely chary of adverse and limiting criticism, and would never dream of pulling a bad poem to pieces for the sake of giving his powers of discrimination an airing. This difference has come about by reason of a subsidiary social and educational purpose in Richards's work—the purpose of providing a defence against the flood of trash and corrupted values that now besiege culture on every side. Heaven knows the defence is needed; but it is a matter of some difficulty to know how far literary studies can go in this direction without losing their own integrity. We cannot discuss this question here; but it is true that in the large body of writing in English that has followed directly on Richards's work we find consequences of this attitude that are not particularly admirable. The embattled stance towards bad writing tends to become habitual, tends to extend itself to the good, and to preclude a more generous acceptance. *Scrutiny's* inveterate hostility towards most of the creative literature of its own time is a case in point. To use Richards's own terminology, doctrinal adhesions and stock responses of a more or less sociological kind find it too easy to obtain a lodgement in literary criticism conducted under these auspices.

Quite evidently this was far from Richards's intention. But it was accidentally encouraged by the non-historical nature of his inquiry. The contributors to the *Practical Criticism* experiment were required to spin their judgments out of their own entrails, without any help from the sense of cultural tradition, so strong in the best Continental style-study. And this leads us to ask how far literary judgment and interpretation, divorced from history and cultural tradition, are possible at all. George Watson has remarked that all that was really proved by *Practical Criticism* is that unhistorical reading is bad reading. And making all allowance for the special nature of the investigation, I think we must give some weight to this. We are invited to shake our heads over the misinterpretations of Donne's sonnet 'At the round earth's imagined corners'; but a good deal of it is due to ignorance that was forced upon the commentators by the circumstances of the inquiry. True, it would not happen now; a comparable audience would probably know the poem; but at a period when seventeenth-century religious poetry had been little studied, and was certainly not part of the equipment of the ordinary student, no adequate set of comments could have resulted.

It is not, as rather seems to be suggested by the tone of the discussion in *Practical Criticism*, a matter of such information as a footnote could supply—about beliefs concerning the Last Judgment, etc.—though indeed a good deal of such information is needed. It is at least some understanding of a whole state of mind and climate of feeling that is required. To read the poem out of its context is not to read it at all. And it cannot be denied that Richards's work has in subsequent educational practice often been misinterpreted, and has inadvertently encouraged ill-prepared reading of this kind, and even led to the belief (more evident amongst students a few years ago than it is now) that literary study is a mere orgy of rootless opinion, sanctioned by a few procedural tricks. But even so the balance is heavily on the credit side. The sense of mere helplessness in stylistic inquiry has disappeared; some notion of how to tackle questions of literary interpretation is widespread; and this can be seen everywhere, from the work of students, through general criticism, up to studies of the highest scholarly kind. In fact, Richards had a lesson to teach and a great number of people have learnt it. That it has not proved a cure for all our cultural ills is another matter.

William Empson

Practical Criticism is obviously a prolegomena to style-study rather than an example of it. The work of William Empson both extends Richards's methodological inquiries and affords some massive examples of the method in action. The exemplification comes first. Empson's first book, *Seven Types of Ambiguity*, was written directly under Richards's influence, much of it indeed while Richards was still teaching him in Cambridge; and it is essentially the application of Richards's method to a particular literary problem. It is what we called in the previous chapter the investigation of a special expressive device, but it is a very extended one. By the time Empson has finished with it, the special device becomes almost a fundamental feature of all poetic language. Richards's analysis of meaning obviously leans towards the idea of a composite reaction to a single utterance. The sense, for instance, may seem to lead us in one direction, the feeling in another, and this may be enriching, not confusing. Under the heading *ambiguity*, Empson greatly develops this idea. 'I propose', he says, 'to use the word in an extended sense and shall think relevant to my subject any verbal nuance, however slight, which gives room for alternative reactions to the same piece of language.' The result is a rich and detailed exemplification of the possibilities of multiple meaning in poetic language. It caused a good deal of alarm when it first appeared. Empson is more ingeniously intelligent than any of his critics; he takes a slightly fantastic delight in verbal analysis; and, as he says in the Preface to the Second Edition, he erected the ignoring of tact into a point of honour. But when the dust settled some years later it turned out that his main principles had been quietly absorbed into the canon of modern literary criticism. The words 'tension', 'paradox', 'irony', which have done such heavy duty in the last thirty years are all adaptations of the Empsonian 'ambiguity'.

The common objections to the procedure were that the ingenuities were perversely pursued for their own sake, and that the analysis left a passage or a poem in pieces without reconstituting its totality. The first is false, the second sometimes true, but perhaps inevitable. The book is a commando raid on the ineffable, or on what conventional criticism has been content to regard as ineffable. Again, a few sentences from the Preface to the Second Edition explain perfectly justly what is going on:

I was frequently puzzled in considering my examples. . . . I felt sure the example was beautiful and that I had broadly speaking reacted to it correctly. But I did not at all know what had happened in this reaction; I did not know why the example was beautiful. And it seemed to me that I was able in some cases partly to explain my feeling to myself by teasing out the meanings of the text. Yet these meanings when teased out (in a major example) were too complicated to be remembered together as if in one glance of the eye; they had to be followed each in turn, as possible alternative reactions to the passage; and indeed there is no doubt that some readers sometimes do only get part of the full intention.

Space forbids any illustration of the working of his method; and in any case the book is familiar. I want to point out here, however, that for all the difference of tone and manner the method is essentially the same as that of Spitzer and Alonso—an intuitive grasp of the work, followed by an analytical attempt to show how the intuition was arrived at. Of course, the methods of analysis are very different from those of the Continental scholars. Auerbach, Spitzer and Alonso make far more systematic use of the history of the language and of general cultural history. Empson remains more closely focused on the reader's mind. But, like Alonso, he believed that the reaction in the reader's mind, if it is correct and not merely capricious, reconstitutes the reaction in the mind of the author at the time of creation. 'If critics are not to put up some pretence of understanding the feeling of the author they must condemn themselves to contempt.' Empson's reactions it must be confessed have sometimes been capricious, and historical scholars have sometimes been able to catch him out. This does not, however, invalidate his procedure.

The Structure of Complex Words is clearly continuous with the earlier book. It contains a detailed critique of some of Richards's views, offers another approach to replace them, and gives some admirable fully developed examples of this apparatus in action. The point in Richards's work which Empson takes up has already been mentioned. It is the tendency to bundle all aspects of meaning that are not sense under the head of 'emotion'. Empson takes exception to this. To describe complex metaphorical and figurative language in poetry as having 'purely emotive value' is to give an inadequate account both of what it achieves and how it works. He proceeds to analyse most of what Richards calls 'emotive' as modification or subsidiary direction of sense. What Richards calls the 'pseudo-statements' of poetry are in fact ways of stating something, not merely attempts at manipulating the reader's feelings. Empson does not deny the role of feeling, but he sets himself to answer the difficult yet elementary question of how the feelings get into words, if they do get in; or how the words indicate their presence, if the feelings merely accompany the words.

He first attempted to separate various entities in the habitual uses of a single word—particularly *senses*, *implications*, *emotions* and *moods*. He then goes on to show how these separate entities interact with each other— how a word can apparently carry a doctrine or direct opinion. It does this, he says, by various kinds of equations, which are then described, illustrated and commented on. Here I abandon the attempt to summarize; the inquirer must read Chapter 2 of the book for himself. Empson devises a symbolism to present these entities and relations; and the system develops numerous offshoots and parentheses. I do not doubt for a moment that he is describing something which really goes on, and that he accounts for many ways of conveying meaning that have not been accounted for before; but as it is presented I find the argument difficult to follow. The symbolism is, I think, ill-chosen and unmemorable, there are too many aspects to be considered, and what needs to be sub-divided or presented in tabular form is done as a continuous argument, so that it is too easy to lose the thread. Perhaps I am exceptionally stupid or exceptionally lazy, but I cannot keep so many balls in the air at once. There are hardly any local obscurities; the writing is always lucid in detail, but I lose the sense of the whole. I suspect I am not alone in this; and it does raise the question of how far a literary argument can depart from ordinary literary methods without denying itself to precisely those readers who are likely to seek illumination from it.

However, the theoretical chapters are only part of the book. The rest consists of extensive essays in which the method is applied. Key words in certain works are examined and their various permutations and combinations are seen in the light of the whole work in question. Examples are: 'wit' in the *Essay on Criticism*, 'honest' in *Othello*, 'sense' and 'sensibility' in various contexts, 'sense' in *Measure for Measure*. These inquiries are stylistics in the strictest sense; they start from close verbal analysis and end in controlled literary interpretation. We may agree or disagree, but the argument is generally close and continuous and we are not left with the awkward feeling common in reading Continental stylistics that there is a gap between positive linguistic observation and highly speculative literary conclusions. One cannot suppose that this Empsonian shorthand is ever likely to become popular reading; but there is no reason why the method in a less concentrated form should not be perfectly available to others; and it certainly leads into wide stretches of unexplored territory. We often hear about how semantics ought to assist criticism; these brilliant and deeply thought essays of Empson's are almost the only places I know of where it has really done so to much purpose.

So I believe that Empson's work is immensely important and that it has not yet had its full effect. He has to a certain extent become the victim of his own endowments. Trained as a mathematician before he turned to literature, with a considerable interest in the sort of problems that symbolic logic investigates, a poet himself, he brings to his critical work an equipment that the average literary student cannot easily cope with. Add to this a few passionate convictions, occasional bouts of ferocity, a vigorous comic sense, and we have a mixture that the academic appetite finds fairly indigestible. Yet it is too much like hard work to have a very wide appeal outside the academy. I suspect that literary studies must go on digesting it for some time yet.

John Holloway

English style-studies do not show much continuity; they are rather a succession of fresh starts. An entirely new direction is found in John Holloway's book, *The Victorian Sage*. It does not take off from the work of Richards and Empson, and it owes nothing to Continental stylistics. Yet it clearly is stylistics—a study of the detailed verbal organization by which larger literary effects are produced. As Richards approached literature from semantics and experimental psychology, so Holloway approaches it from philosophy—Oxford philosophy of the 1940's. Richards's point of view has an evident kinship with early logical positivism. Early logical positivism was concerned to distinguish meaningful statements from statements that were strictly nonsense (not nonsense = rubbish, but nonsense = non-sense). By Holloway's time the direction of interest had changed. The realm of non-sense continued to be thickly populated, and it obviously included most of the things in which men take a passionate interest. Even if statements of this class were not subject to verification, they continued to be made, were made for some reason and presumably had some significance. So a later kind of verbal analysis set itself to inquire what these significances are. This is roughly the change from early to late Wittgenstein; and it is from this later viewpoint that Holloway's work starts.

The great Victorian sages, Carlyle, Newman, Arnold and some of the novelists, all express notions of great scope and generality about the world, man's situation in it and how he should live. Yet they all seem to feel themselves dispensed from the burden of proof. Their arguments are not logical or empirical demonstrations; to a greater or less degree, all of them deal in vast oracular assumptions, large assertions, 'broad sweeping gestures, hints thrown out, suggestions which leave us quite uncertain about their detailed import'. They exercise and have continued to exercise a pervading power. The question that Holloway sets himself to answer is how this power is exercised, what methods supply the place of proof, of logical argument, of empirical demonstration in writing of this kind. Obviously this is a matter of great literary importance. The case of the Victorian sage is particularly well marked, but it is not unique; and these characteristic techniques of persuasion are liable to be found in literature at most times. Holloway confines himself to a particular phase of a particular historical period; but the questions he raises and the answers he provides have a wide application; they concern the status and the procedure of that vast body of speculative, persuasive and hortatory literature, neither formally philosophical nor strictly scientific, that is found at all periods.

Again, it is impossible to summarize the book at all comprehensively; the discussion is very close and impossible to generalize. Since the sage or thinker is not working to the rules of any formal discipline, the directing force behind his writing tends to be his own temperament and his own experience. This is particularly marked in the case of Matthew Arnold, of which Holloway gives a subtle and penetrating analysis. Arnold's favourite method is to exhibit his own personality as an example of the virtues that he is recommending; and he uses irony partly indeed as a weapon against his opponents, but partly as irony directed against himself, to disinfect this presentation of his own personality from complacency and self-importance. If disinterestedness, urbanity and amenity are to be pressed upon the British public, the very texture of all Arnold's writing must exhibit these virtues, and the process of persuasion is more like a face-to-face encounter with a person in actual life than a formal argument, the capacity for which Arnold is always disclaiming. Another of his methods is repeated and cumulative quotation from his adversaries, by which process a particular response, this time unfavourable, to their attitudes and temperaments is built up. An extension of this is the creation of imaginary personalities to be the bearers both of his own attitudes and those of his adversaries. And here Arnold joins hands with Carlyle, who exhibits even more strongly this tendency to dramatize an argument. In his case it is a function of his overwhelming sense of movement and activity, of a world full of variety, development and burgeoning life. His vocabulary and his metaphors, both of which Holloway illustrates very fully, exhibit this quality at every turn. Newman is examined in the same way—his forms of argument, his use of suggestive examples and his imagery are all discussed.

These three essays do something new. They give an analysis of informal unprofessional philosophical writing from the point of view of a linguistic philosopher. Holloway is not much interested in the validity of the arguments (had he been, he would have been obliged to say that some of them are remarkably slippery): it is their methods that interest him. And he demonstrates the existence of a method that can be examined and described, in literary areas that had formerly been extremely resistant to analysis. The three remaining chapters of the book are on novelists, Disraeli, George Eliot and Hardy, whom Holloway sees also as sages—quite appropriately within his terms of reference. But here his own method tends to take a different direction. As is usual in criticism of a novel, it is the larger features—character, incident, description—that engages his interest, and the linguistic structure is less attended to. There is some examination of images and descriptive passages, but a good deal of these essays is close and intelligent general criticism rather than stylistics.

Stephen Ullmann

We can contrast Holloway's treatment of the novel with that in Stephen Ullmann's work—*Style in the French Novel* and *The Image in the Modern French Novel*. Ullmann writes in English, but his procedure is closely allied to that of Continental stylistics. Much of his work has been on semantics. The introductory chapter of *Style in the French Novel* (together with a later book, *Language and Style*) gives a valuable compendium of current stylistic methods and problems; indeed, it is the best general introduction to the subject in English. In general, Ullmann starts from linguistic observations and tries to indicate how the gap between linguistic and literary study can be bridged. Unlike Spitzer, he advances no comprehensive theory of the relation between linguistics and literary history, but he has made a number of separate studies of particular stylistic questions. For instance, the essay on reported speech in Flaubert takes up the question of the *style indirect libre*, gives a report of preceding discussions of the matter and carries them a stage further. Other essays in the same volume deal with the attempt of French novelists of the nineteenth century to introduce local colour into their work, and with certain syntactical constructions in the work of the Goncourts which can be seen as parallel to impressionist techniques in painting. These are evidently parts of a large tendency in the nineteenth-century French novel— to introduce a more colourful and expressive style into prose fiction—a tendency which has gone much farther in our own century. Ullmann confines himself pretty much to specific and limited questions, but his books also give extensive and valuable bibliographical indications, often to works that are not generally known to English readers. We can learn from them how much more there is to be done in this field, and in what directions further inquiries can be pursued.

Donald Davie

Last, I want to refer to two books by Donald Davie, unique and isolated pieces of work, both dealing with matters of great general significance. They are *Purity of Diction in English Verse* and *Articulate Energy*. The first deals with the diction and the second with the syntax of English poetry. These works are isolated because their starting-point is neither linguistics nor conventional stylistic criticism; they arise rather from Davie's own concerns as a poet. Even when they deal with matters that have often been discussed in a special technical vocabulary, they make very sparing use of linguistic terminology. They show indeed what in the view of many people, myself included, needs to be shown—that linguistic matters can be properly discussed in the traditional language of literary criticism.

Purity of Diction has as its point of departure a particular phase in the history of modern English poetry— a reaction (in itself probably a minor affair) against the self-consciously concrete, image-packed style that was the English heritage of symbolism. As a result of what can roughly be called the imagist propaganda of Pound and Eliot, it had become almost dogma in the thirties and forties that the language of poetry must be inveterately concrete, that the prime weapon of poetry is the image. Davie has no difficulty in showing that historically this is a good deal less than certain; and he sets out to illustrate the virtues of another currently neglected kind of diction, a diction characterized by a cool exactitude, often abstract, rather than by the desire to hand over immediate physical sensation. His intention is partly polemical and to that extent aside from stylistics; but in the course of pressing his argument he gives extremely sensitive and original analyses of poetic language from the seventeenth to the twentieth century.

It was also a received idea that the first necessity for poetry in the earlier part of this century was the establishment of an appropriate modern poetic diction. The effect of Davie's slightly sceptical inquiries was to remove some of the emphasis from diction. The question was then where the emphasis was to be put. The answer to this comes in Davie's next book, *Articulate Energy*, which is about poetic syntax. If we begin to doubt the absolute primacy of a vivid and sharply-coloured diction, it becomes clear that the principal agent of poetic power is syntax—syntax in the widest sense. The effect of imagist doctrine had been to depreciate syntax, even in extreme cases to abolish it altogether. A mere parataxis of striking images was to take its place. As Davie uses the word, it is not simply syntax in the grammatical sense, not simply *ordonnance* in the interests of lucid and effective arrangement. It means the whole skeletal and muscular structure of poetic language, as the only possible instrument of poetic energy. The word 'poetic' is an important qualification, for the variety of syntax possible in poetry is far wider than in prose. Davie illustrates this with an impressive range of discussions both of current theory and past practice. Again there is a polemical purpose; but even if this should come to seem less relevant than it once was, the book remains immensely illuminating. These two books illustrate very clearly that whatever contribution linguistics can bring to literary studies there is no substitute for literary understanding and literary ability. And that is not a bad note to end this chapter on.

5

Conclusion:
limits and possibilities

It will be apparent from what has been said already that the contribution of linguistics to style-study is strictly limited. It is virtually confined to semantics and syntax. Many of the positivist linguists of a now slightly outdated school regarded semantics as only doubtfully a part of their discipline, and semantics has therefore been rather apart from the main body of modern linguistics. Much of the modern study of syntax is remote from literary interests, and for many of its practitioners (Chomsky, for instance) literature is only an epiphenomenon.

There is a fundamental reason for this. Modern structural linguistics sets out to study language as a general human phenomenon, and to evolve a set of concepts that will describe any language. A linguist who is studying, say, modern English has to keep this whole explanatory scheme in mind. Stylistics is in quite a different position. It studies particular works in a particular language. A student of style in the modern French novel is not at all helped by remembering the linguistic habits of the Hopi Indians. And even the French language is of interest to him within narrow limits. *La langue*, the public, shared system of the language, its phonemic, morphemic

H

and syntactical structure, is for him a datum, not an object of investigation. He is concerned only with *la parole*, a series of individual communicative acts, individual applications of the code. Great harm is done to fruitful collaboration between linguistics and literary studies by linguists who wish to foist on literature a whole battery of apparatus and a whole array of accomplishments that are quite irrelevant to its purpose.

In fact, Continental stylistics arose out of an older school of historical linguistics. This was indeed the linguistics of a particular language, or group of languages; and so in an obvious sense it was closer to style-study. Even here much of it was irrelevant. It is frequent to find, for example, in the work of Spitzer fossils of historical philology that serve him as a starting-point, but have little real connection with what he ultimately wants to say. And the school of Richards shows that the starting-point could be quite different. But the fact remains that literature is a linguistic structure, and some awareness of the nature of language would seem to be essential to the student of literature. There is an obvious value in even so much (or so little) linguistics as would remind the literary student that all literary communication is achieved by linguistic means, that these means can be described, and that linguistic techniques can alert him to features that would otherwise have passed unnoticed. The absence of this awareness in *Practical Criticism* and its progeny has undoubtedly been damaging. The emphasis on uninspectable events in the reader's mind, and his 'attitudes' and emotions, has led much literary study into an orgy of unsubstantiated opinion—amateur philosophizing, amateur sociology, and propaganda for whatever code of morals the individual critic happens to support. This is not to say that such work can have no value: it approximates to the activity of the Victorian sage, and it requires long experience and great general powers. But it cannot be a progressive study; it is persuasion rather than knowledge; and it is a poor educational foundation. One cannot really run a School of Prophecy. Stylistics makes more modest claims: that it can be the systematic (I will not say scientific) study of literary expression; that within limits it can increase knowledge; that this knowledge can be consolidated, and within limits communicated to others.

What are these limits? One is the limit of natural aptitude, the capacity for receiving intuitions from works of literature. About this there is nothing to say. The other is that stylistics, however extended, can never cover the whole field of literary study. Much that literary students are interested in consists of larger units than style-study can cope with—plot, character, and the *ordonnance* of ideas; and without becoming 'the gay sporting-ground of incompetence', in Spitzer's phrase, literary study can attack these larger structures direct, short-circuiting the approach through language and style. The methods are different, but failure of communication between them is not necessary. Empson, who has approached Shakespeare through language, has said that the Shakespearian critic he most admires is Bradley.

It seems likely that modern linguistics is developing in ways that will take it farther away from literature— hence the old-fashioned air of most of the linguistic references in this book; but mention must be made to one move in the contrary direction. I mean the holy alliance between linguistics and anthropology associated with the work of Lévi-Strauss. Lévi-Strauss is an anthropologist, and of this, his real field, I can say nothing. But the essence of his work is to discover a common principle in all human thought—in myth, primitive religion, kinship patterns, equally with the thinking of

modern man. The emphasis is on thought; and the affective element, the psychology of the passions that we
associate with Freud, is depreciated. Part of Lévi-Strauss's
structural organon is derived from Saussurean linguistics,
with additions from one of the most distinguished linguists of the next generation, the Russo-American Roman
Jakobson. A particularly important principle is that of
binary opposition, the choice between a pair of alterna-
tives as the fundamental principle of human thinking.
(It is often difficult to tell whether this is put forward as
part of the nature of things, or simply as a model, a heu-
ristic convenience.) And as anthropology has borrowed
from linguistics, so literary thinking in its turn is inclined to borrow from both. There has been a wide extension of quasi-anthopological ideas, an enthusiastic and
often quite irresponsible application of methods drawn
from one discipline to others with which it is not evidently related. In French criticism 'structuralism' has
become a magic word. Roland Barthes, its principal
spokesman, professes a science of semiology, a key to all
cultural codes, whether they are linguistic or not. But he
is also a critic and writer on style. His *Essais Critiques*
appear to the outsider a rather belated discussion of
modern critical methods already more fully worked out
in Anglo-American writing, together with a little communication theory—the whole boiled up into a highly
flavoured stew. His book on Racine displays under the
name of 'structuralism' an assortment of familiar but
erratically employed Freudian ideas. It has been effec-
tively, but rather stuffily, criticized by Raymond Picard. In
Le degré zéro de l'ecriture Barthes is nearer to stylistics
with an analysis of neutral or 'styleless' writing. There
is a ferment here that recalls the controversies of the
forties about the New Criticism in America. Some of
it is mere froth; but there is also a host of new ideas,

though they are more likely to prove fruitful in philosophical criticism than in stylistics.

A more serious instance of structuralism applied to literature, and one much nearer the fountain-head, is a joint study of Baudelaire's sonnet 'Les chats' by Jakobson and Lévi-Strauss. Such a collaboration cannot be without importance. The point of view is made clear in the introductory paragraph:

It may seem surprising that an anthropological review should publish a study devoted to a French poem of the nineteenth century. However, the explanation is simple: if a linguist and an ethnologist have thought fit to unite their efforts to understand what a sonnet of Baudelaire was made of, it is because they have found themselves independently confronted with complementary problems. in poetical works the linguist discerns structures that bear a striking analogy with those that the analysis of myths reveals to the ethnologist.

There follows a minute formal analysis of the poem, comprehending the stanza-form, rhyme-scheme, the phonological structure and the semantic structure. The closeness of the observation, and its justness, cannot be doubted, as is never the case with Barthes. There is an obvious gain in perception of detail which the normal literary student would hardly have noticed; but it remains an open question how great is the gain for literary understanding. All that is demonstrated by this in some ways impressive piece of analysis is that many structures actually present in a work of literature are without literary importance, and that some things of literary importance cannot be represented in structural terms at all.

Every study has its own end, and therefore a relative autonomy within its own sphere. In literary study there can be no substitute for literary intelligence. But every study has its external relations: it may be part of a larger whole; it may have multifarious links with other activities. It is hard to see literary study as part of a larger whole; and its links with other activities have probably been too many and too unregulated for its own good. The literary philosophy and the literary sociology that we have mentioned are cases in point. One contact that is indispensable is that of literature with language, of criticism with linguistics; and it obviously needs more disinterested investigation than it has had. This is not, or should not be, a take-over bid by either side; it is the exploration of a common frontier. Stylistics is the border area between these two studies, and as yet it is neither adequately mapped nor firmly settled. It would be a mistake to underrate the difficulties.

The first is that every branch of study in modern conditions makes such huge demands. The literary canon presented to a student of English literature is vastly enlarged since the old days, when it ran from Chaucer to Wordsworth. Even if we neglect transitory novelties (and we probably do not want to, for they may speak to our condition) the range of necessary critical ideas is far wider than it used to be. And no one can be satisfied with a literary education confined to a single language. To attain any real competence as what was once called 'a man of letters' is a long and exacting process; and it can hardly be combined with a long and exacting process of quite a different kind. Modern linguistics is a highly developed and complex science, with many branches, with its own intellectual apparatus, and a frame of reference that only overlaps with literary study in a small and peripheral area. What is more, the state of mind in which the two studies are pursued is radically different. The linguist aims to describe the object of his investigation as fully and explicitly as possible, without any ambiguity or appeal to intuition. The literary student finds complete description superfluous or stultifying, often values the suggestive rather than the explicit, and is tolerant of diverse interpretations. For the linguist value resides in the completeness and exactitude of his descriptions; the actual material he works on may be a mere *corpus vile* used for experimental purposes. For the literary student value resides in the work of art under consideration; description and interpretation are ancillary and subservient to a kind of contemplative understanding that is essentially independent of these activities.

So I think it quite idle to suppose that literary criticism and linguistics can ever be a united field, though they can form brief alliances for special purposes. The special purposes are likely to be those of the student of literature. I have never, in such reading of linguistics as I have done, noticed any occasion when the linguist has wanted to avail himself of literary knowledge. There are many occasions when the literary student, especially the student of style, wants to make use of linguistic techniques and linguistic knowledge. But he will hardly be equipped with the full range of linguistic skills, and he will probably make brief raids on whatever parts of linguistics suit his purpose. There is no reason to suppose that style-study will be willing to follow wherever the technical exigencies of linguistics happen to lead. As time goes on, it is just as likely that literary thinking about style will be influenced by a general 'science of signs', a semiology less eccentric and trivial than that of Barthes. It may be more affected by communication theory, some of whose concepts seem admirably adapted to literary use. Works of literature are expressed in language; they are systems of signs; they are communications. Ideas drawn from the sciences that preside over these several areas can all contribute to literary study. But literary works are also works of art of a unique kind, and their proper study has its own methods and its own ends. It even has its own public, different from that of the more specialized sciences. However esoteric literary studies may become, they must fail of their object unless their results ultimately filter through to the intelligent common reader, and unless they are expressible in something like the language of common life.

Select Bibliography

Short notes are given on works not discussed in the text.

ALONSO, A., 'The Stylistic Interpretation of Literary Texts', *Modern Language Notes*, LVII (1942), 489–96.

A liberal-minded manifesto for stylistics as a literary activity.

ALONSO, D., *Poesia española; ensayo de metodos y limites estilisticos*, Madrid, 1950.

AUERBACH, E., *Mimesis: the Representation of Reality in Western Literature*, trans. Willard Trask, Princeton, 1953.

BAILEY, R. W. and BURTON, D. M., *English Stylistics: a Bibliography*, M.I.T., 1968.

The only full critical bibliography of English stylistics. Much needed.

BALLY, C., *Traité de stylistique française*, 3rd edn., Paris, 1951.
—— *Le langage et la vie*, 3rd edn., Geneva, 1951.

BARTHES, R., *Writing Degree Zero*, trans. Annette Lavers and Colin Smith, 1967 (*Le Degré Zéro de l'ecriture*, Paris, 1953).
—— *Essais Critiques*, Paris, 1964.
—— *Sur Racine*, Paris, 1963.

BLOOMFIELD, L., *Language*, New York, 1953.

A standard comprehensive handbook of linguistics, now partly superseded by Hockett.

BOOTH, W. C., *The Rhetoric of Fiction*, Chicago and London, 1961.

A pioneering study of the expressive resources of the novel, especially of the role of the narrator.

CRESSOT, M., *Le style et les techniques: précis d'analyse stylistique*, Paris, 1947.

DAVIE, D., *Purity of Diction in English Verse*, London: Chatto & Windus, 1952; rev. edn., 1967.

—— *Articulate Energy*, London: Routledge & Kegan Paul, 1955.

DOUBROVSKY, S., *Pourquoi la nouvelle critique?*, Paris, 1967.
A defence of Barthes and the French 'new criticism' generally.

EMPSON, W., *Seven Types of Ambiguity*, London: Chatto & Windus, 1930; rev. edn., 1947.

—— *The Structure of Complex Words*, London: Chatto & Windus, 1951.

ENKVIST, N. E., SPENCER, J., and GREGORY, M. J., *Linguistics and Style*, Oxford, 1964.
Useful opening essay on defining style.

FOWLER, R. (ed.), *Essays on Style and Language*, London: Routledge & Kegan Paul, 1966.
A collection of essays attempting to explore 'an area where linguistics and literary criticism overlap'. Not notably successful from the literary point of view.

GOURMONT, R. DE, *Le problème du style*, Paris, 1902.
An early classic in this field. The principal essay in the collection is a polemic against mechanical and external ideas of style.

HAMILTON, G. R., *The Tell-tale Article: a Critical Approach to Modern Poetry*, London: Heinemann, 1949.

HATZFELD, H., 'Stylistic Criticism as Art-minded Philology', Yale French Studies, II (1949), 1–9.

—— *A Critical Bibliography of the New Stylistics, applied to the Romance Languages, 1900–52*; Chapel Hill, N.C., 1953.
A comprehensive bibliography, with very full discussion, of stylistic work on the Romance languages. This is not only an indispensable tool, but amounts to a critical work in its own right.

HOCKETT, C. F., *A Course in Modern Linguistics*, New York, 1958.
The best and most up-to-date general handbook.

HOLLOWAY, J., *The Victorian Sage: Studies in Argument*, 1953.

JAKOBSON, R., and LEVI-STRAUSS, C., ' "Les Chats" de Charles Baudelaire', *L'homme: revue française d'anthropologie*, II, 1 (1962).

LODGE, D., *Language of Fiction: Essays in Criticism and Verbal Analysis of the English Novel*, 1966.

Particularly useful introduction on the novel as a linguistic structure.

MILES, J., *Eras and Modes in English Poetry*, Berkeley, 1964.

MURRY, J. M., *The Problem of Style*, 1922.

A general discussion, rather loose and unsystematic by later standards, but containing some valuable observations.

NOWOTTNY, W., *The Language Poets Use*, 1962.

A sensitive and original account of poetic language, using linguistic insights in the interests of literary understanding.

PICARD, R., *Nouvelle critique où nouvelle imposture*, Paris, 1965.

An attack on Barthes and the French 'new criticism' in general.

RICHARDS, I. A., *Principles of Literary Criticism*, 1924.

—— *Practical Criticism*, 1929.

—— *Interpretation in Teaching*, 1938.

SAUSSURE, F. DE, *Cours de linguistique générale*, 5th edn., Paris, 1955.

SAYCE, R. A., *Style in French Prose: a Method of Analysis*, 1953.

A systematic procedure for the analysis of prose—too systematic, probably, for most literary purposes.

SCHERER, J., *L'expression littéraire dans l'œuvre de Mallarmé*, Paris, 1947.

SEBEOK, T. A., (ed.), *Style in Language*, New York and London, 1960.

Report of a joint conference of linguists and literary critics: a few articles of merit, but on the whole profoundly depressing, and contains more nauseous jargon than any similar work known to me.

SPITZER, L., *Linguistics and Literary History*, Princeton, 1948.

—— *Essays on English and American Literature*, Princeton, 1962.

—— *Stilstudien*, Marburg, 1928.

Style in Prose Fiction: English Institute Essays 1958, New York, 1959.

A collection of essays: valuable introductory essay by R. N. Ohmann on the concept of style.

THIBAUDET, A., *Gustave Flaubert, 1821–80; sa vie, ses romans, son style*, Paris, 1922.

Admirable chapter on Flaubert's style.

ULLMANN, S., *Style in the French Novel*, 1957; 2nd edn., 1964.

Useful introduction on stylistics in general, a sound working bibliography, and further very extensive bibliographical indications in the notes.

—— *The Image in the Modern French Novel*, London: Cambridge University Press, 1960.

VOSSLER, K., *Medieval Culture: an Introduction to Dante and His Times (Die göttliche Komödie)*, trans. W. C. Lawton, London: Constable, 1929.

—— *The Spirit of Language in Civilization*, trans. O. Oeser, London: Kegan Paul, 1932.

WIMSATT, W. K., *The Prose Style of Samuel Johnson*, New Haven, 1941.

YULE, G. U., *The Statistical Interpretation of Literary Vocabulary*, London: Cambridge University Press, 1944.